Managing teams in the Age of AI

A step-by-step guide for managing technical personas, process transformation, and fostering innovation

Ankur Agrawal

bpb

www.bpbonline.com

First Edition 2025

Copyright © BPB Publications, India

ISBN: 978-93-65898-361

To View Complete
BPB Publications Catalogue
Scan the QR Code:

www.bpbonline.com

Dedicated to

My esteemed late father, Shri S. K. Agrawal

and

my loving son, Aryan

About the Author

Ankur Agrawal has been working in the software industry for over 25 years, including close to 18 years in various leadership roles in notable companies such as Microsoft, Salesforce and Flipkart. He has explored a large landscape of software engineering and leadership space, ranging from low-level embedded systems, operating systems, device drivers, networking protocols, to large-scale distributed systems, cloud services, and AI platforms. He has built and led large teams comprising software engineers, data scientists, and product managers. Ankur also had the opportunity to mentor and coach hundreds of engineers and leaders. He has extensively shared his experience in the leadership domain as a speaker and ardent writer of articles on professional platforms. In this book, he shares his knowledge and insights in a comprehensive manner to help the leaders with their journey in a systematic manner, especially in the rapidly evolving world of artificial intelligence.

About the Reviewers

* **Shilpa Lulla** is a seasoned engineering leader at Microsoft, leading global teams and building AI-powered platforms. Her work focuses on intelligent systems, responsible innovation, and real-world impact, driven by the belief that technology should empower people. With over two decades of experience, she has held senior roles at Honeywell, Inovalon, and Cornerstone OnDemand, driving transformation across various technology domains. Shilpa has also established satellite development centers that thrive as hubs of engineering excellence.

  Her journey is rooted in curiosity, resilience, and a passion for solving meaningful problems through technology. She is an advocate for thoughtful design, agile execution, and continuous learning. Shilpa is dedicated to mentoring future leaders and technologists, bringing empathy and commitment to inclusive growth.

  This book resonates deeply with her values. In an era where artificial intelligence is reshaping how we work, lead, and live, Shilpa believes that thoughtful leadership is more critical than ever. She believes that contributing to this book has been a meaningful opportunity to reflect on what it takes to lead with purpose, empathy, and vision in a time of rapid technological change and uncertain times.

* **Apoorv Malmane** is a principal engineer at VMware by Broadcom, where he leads global efforts in network virtualization, cloud infrastructure, and enterprise security. With over a decade of experience driving innovation at scale, Apoorv has played a pivotal role in designing, optimizing and securing high-performance virtualized environments for Fortune 500 organizations worldwide. He is widely recognized for his deep expertise in virtualization technologies. His unique solutions have directly influenced product development and improved security posture across global deployments.

As a senior member of IEEE and a technical reviewer, Apoorv continues to contribute to the broader engineering community. He has judged prestigious industry awards, served on advisory committees, and delivered technical training sessions across multiple countries, empowering professionals with cutting-edge troubleshooting skills and architectural best practices. He has also contributed to the development of expert-level security certification exams. He is actively involved in mentoring teams, guiding quality assurance efforts, and driving improvements in software reliability.

His contributions extend beyond engineering execution—he is a thought leader, mentor, and strategic advisor dedicated to advancing the state of enterprise technology and inspiring the next generation of engineers.

❖ **Pradeep Kumar Muthukamatchi** is a principal cloud architect at Microsoft with over 13 years of IT experience, specializing in AI and cloud transformation. He empowers startups to leverage Azure, integrating intelligent AI solutions and building secure, scalable cloud infrastructures. Recognized as a thought leader, Pradeep's insights are featured on the Forbes Technology Council, and he is a LinkedIn Top Voice in cloud computing.

Beyond his professional role, Pradeep is passionate about mentoring and volunteering. He guides startups through top accelerator programs like *Alchemist Accelerator*, *Lighthouse Labs*, and *Startupbootcamp*, and serves as a technical reviewer for major AI and cloud publications. Pradeep also mentors students globally through initiatives such as Global Mentorship Initiative, AI4ALL, ADPList, and CodePath.

Pradeep excels at translating complex technology into actionable business results, helping organizations navigate the evolving AI-landscape and driving innovation and business success.

Acknowledgement

First and foremost, I want to express my deepest gratitude towards my parents and elders who inculcated the progressive and learning mindset in me to explore the unknown and be positive and solution-oriented even in the most challenging situations. I am also grateful to my family members, who always provided the support system for me to be able to explore my interests and passions.

I would like to thank all the great managers and seniors I was lucky to have worked with throughout my career. They set such great examples and provided me with numerous opportunities to grow, which helped me in acquiring the skills and mindset essential to excel in the art of leadership and professionalism.

I would also like to acknowledge the valuable contributions of my colleagues throughout my many years in the tech industry. It has been a great privilege to be part of their circle and learn so many valuable lessons in building and running exceptional teams and organizations.

I am also grateful to BPB Publications for their guidance and expertise in bringing this book to fruition. It was a long journey of revising this book, with valuable participation and collaboration of reviewers, technical experts, and editors.

Finally, I would like to thank all the readers who have taken an interest in my book and for their support in making it a reality. Your encouragement has been invaluable.

Preface

Artificial intelligence is not just the latest buzzword, but is something that has challenged the fundamentals of how work gets done and what it means to be a human worker. The role of a software engineer is rapidly being re-shaped and re-defined by the rising capabilities of AI in doing many of the most challenging tasks, previously considered possible only by human intelligence. As a result, the role of a manager is also at an interesting juncture where they need to rapidly repivot and evolve to lead in these exciting and challenging times.

The role managers are expected to play in this transformation is more important than ever for the success of engineers, teams, and organizations. They will be pivotal in transitioning the industry through this unprecedented revolution for continued success and growth. They are expected to continue to lead with empathy and demonstrate efficiency and agility in various ways.

The managers will learn a lot of new learnings and acquire new skills as they embark on this unknown and unpredictable journey. This book covers the various aspects of the role of a manager and how one can think about reshaping their mojo as a manager in order to excel in the age of AI and a transformative world in general! This book attempts to lend a helping hand to both new and experienced managers in leading their teams through the transformation as a result of the AI revolution.

Chapter 1: Foundations of the AI Landscape - Takes a stock of the state of the AI world in various aspects. It sets the context of how AI is coming up in the overall skillset canvas and what the hype is about the workforce context. It attempts to cover the changes and impact AI is bringing to our lives in recent times at an uber level. It comprises a few intuitive examples to help the reader build a broad knowledge base as compared to just a few specific tools or applications they might have heard about in their respective field of work or niche.

Chapter 2: Applications of AI in Your Domain - Provides ways to think about AI's role in a given domain. This chapter helps build another layer in the foundation for the rest of the book, that is, understanding applications of AI in software engineering and the management world. With the help of a few out-of-the-box examples, this chapter provides the reader some food for thought on how to think about the possible applications of AI contextualized to their specific world of existence.

Chapter 3: Type A, the Wide-eyed Ones – Is the first of the three chapters that cover the different types of personas a manager might have in their team when it comes to AI orientation. The process of doing this will help the reader understand the composition of their team better and decide their overall planning and strategy in a much more realistic, tailored, and grounded way. This chapter talks about how the first type of persona in a team might think, what works for them, what does not, as well as the strategy for guiding them along the AI journey in the most effective and organic way.

Chapter 4: Type B, the AI Enthusiasts - Helps the reader learn about the second of the three personas from an AI orientation perspective, the AI enthusiasts. The book covers a few ideas on how to identify this persona, their prominent traits, and behaviors. Then, we discuss the kind of conversation a manager should have with them to learn more, orient them towards the common goal of the team, and leverage their energy and strengths to aid the AI journey of the team.

Chapter 5: Type C, the nAI-sayers - Helps the reader learn about the third of the three personas from an AI orientation perspective, the potentially skeptical ones. The chapter covers ideas on how to identify this persona and their prominent traits and behaviors. There is a special focus on how to address and channelize their potential unfavorable stance on AI. The chapter then looks at ideas on how to create a balanced dialogue and scenario for the maximum impact and a win-win situation for them and the team.

Chapter 6: Plan the Transformation - Aims to help with the preparation for setting up an execution plan and related pieces for AI journey and transformation, starting with a short-term 90-day dash. This chapter builds on top of the context and knowledge built in the previous five chapters in a more comprehensive way. This chapter tries to go beyond the simplistic goal of implementing AI everywhere and instead helps come up with a tailored approach that considers specific needs for the reader and their team.

Chapter 7: Execute the Transformation - Discusses the second phase of the AI journey: a great piece of execution. While a great plan is crucial for such a large-scale and high-stakes transformational journey, the plan can only be fruitful if the execution is up to the mark, to follow that excellent plan! We will look at some of the key mechanisms for great execution in general, with a special focus on the 30-60-90-day period. We will look at this in a generic way and work out a template of sorts, which the reader can apply, depending on their specific narrative, goals, and situation, and have their own version of perfect execution.

Chapter 8: Feedback Loop - Aims to serve as the bridge between the short-term dash and the long-term AI-fied future. In this chapter, we look at some ideas on how to enable the listening and feedback system, to help get the pulse of various key stakeholders and use this to make small or large changes for the follow-up period. We will discuss how to seamlessly get back to steady state, following the 90-day dash while keeping the essence of the changed approach. We discuss the importance and methodology of setting up the feedback loop and how to incorporate this feedback into planning and execution. We also discuss ideas on how to get plugged into advancements in AI as an ongoing practice.

Chapter 9: Beyond the Tactical – Takes up the topic of how to strategize for the long-term existence. We will take a look at how to think from a clean slate point of view and how to position AI as a strategic element in the scheme of things, as opposed to the tactical use of AI to get a set of tasks done. We will talk about how to integrate AI seamlessly into the functioning of our team on various axes, such as communication, decision-making, and a holistic set of goals and success measures. We also try to fathom how to re-imagine our team and product in the new-age AI-first world. The reader will learn a few techniques for combining various goals and outcomes, and how to imbibe them well with AI to accelerate their effectiveness further as a manager and leader.

Chapter 10: Planting Seeds for the Future – This is an attempt to offer food for thought about planting the seeds for the future, both in you as a leader and in the future leaders you might be grooming, against the backdrop of a fast-evolving landscape. We will discuss a few strategies for transforming oneself and the team to become more dynamic and more conducive to similar waves of change that might be coming in the future, not just AI. We will discuss how a manager can orient themselves and their teams for a new way of thinking and operating, and the skills and traits we believe will help prepare oneself and the team for the future.

Errata

We take immense pride in our work at BPB Publications and follow best practices to ensure the accuracy of our content to provide with an indulging reading experience to our subscribers. Our readers are our mirrors, and we use their inputs to reflect and improve upon human errors, if any, that may have occurred during the publishing processes involved. To let us maintain the quality and help us reach out to any readers who might be having difficulties due to any unforeseen errors, please write to us at :

errata@bpbonline.com

Your support, suggestions and feedbacks are highly appreciated by the BPB Publications' Family.

Did you know that BPB offers eBook versions of every book published, with PDF and ePub files available? You can upgrade to the eBook version at www.bpbonline.com and as a print book customer, you are entitled to a discount on the eBook copy. Get in touch with us at :

business@bpbonline.com for more details.

At www.bpbonline.com, you can also read a collection of free technical articles, sign up for a range of free newsletters, and receive exclusive discounts and offers on BPB books and eBooks.

Piracy

If you come across any illegal copies of our works in any form on the internet, we would be grateful if you would provide us with the location address or website name. Please contact us at **business@bpbonline.com** with a link to the material.

If you are interested in becoming an author

If there is a topic that you have expertise in, and you are interested in either writing or contributing to a book, please visit **www.bpbonline.com**. We have worked with thousands of developers and tech professionals, just like you, to help them share their insights with the global tech community. You can make a general application, apply for a specific hot topic that we are recruiting an author for, or submit your own idea.

Reviews

Please leave a review. Once you have read and used this book, why not leave a review on the site that you purchased it from? Potential readers can then see and use your unbiased opinion to make purchase decisions. We at BPB can understand what you think about our products, and our authors can see your feedback on their book. Thank you!

For more information about BPB, please visit **www.bpbonline.com**.

Join our Discord space

Join our Discord workspace for latest updates, offers, tech happenings around the world, new releases, and sessions with the authors:

https://discord.bpbonline.com

Table of Contents

CHAPTER 1
Foundations of the AI Landscape

Introduction

This is the first of the two chapters on embracing the power of **artificial intelligence** (**AI**). In this chapter, we will take a high-level stock of the state of the AI world. We will attempt to set the context of how AI is coming in the overall skillset canvas, and what the hype is about in the workforce context. Throughout the narrative, the attempt is to stay balanced, objective, and rational in the picture being painted.

Structure

This chapter covers the following topics:

- World view of AI
- AI as the new buzzword
- Closer look at the current scenario
- Other side of the story
- World of managers

- Upcoming effects of AI on the horizon
- Ethical considerations of AI
- Responsible AI
- Plagiarism

Objectives

By the end of this chapter, you will have a generic understanding of the situation at present and of the progression in AI, as well as, at an uber level, what kind of changes and impact AI is bringing to our lives, especially recently. There are a few simple examples to help you understand this more broadly than the specific tools or applications you might have heard about in your respective field of work or niche.

World view of AI

In simple terms, AI represents the ability of a machine to exhibit simulated human-like intelligence, such as reasoning or taking decisions. This advent results in it being able to do many of the tasks that, previously, were only possible to be carried out by humans. AI is not a new concept and has been an area of research and in the works over many decades. However, in the last 2 to 3 years, it has reached a breakthrough stage, especially with the leapfrogging of both hardware and software, like **large language models** (**LLM**), **graphical processing units** (**GPU**), and ChatGPT, crossing the threshold of theoretical but non-feasible, to real and accurate. Many of the things previously considered somewhat feasible but a long shot, the new models and solutions have the capability to do that at scale, with excellent precision. This technology is becoming reasonably affordable too and thus is moving within everyone's reach very quickly. In simple terms, AI has grown from an interesting and fun toy to a real and dependable accessory. Previously a toddler, it is now a complete grown-up, educated and a capable adult in the room. Hence, this can formally be considered a revolution in the field of technology and not merely sci-fi fantasy in movies and fictional literature.

Throughout human history, there have been numerous such revolutions, and a lot of the big ones ended up fundamentally re-defining our society and disrupting how humans live and work.

Be it the discovery of electricity, the invention of the telephone, or the arrival of personal computers and smartphones in more recent times. However, what makes the AI revolution million times more powerful is that its applications are not limited to specific tasks or being more of an optional accessory and having a say in only a part of our lives. AI has applications in almost every field, even those only humans could do since they required creativity and non-trivial and not-just-logic-driven decision-making. For instance, AI can now create the most original and beautiful piece of art simply by being given a description of what we want. It can suggest a diagnosis and prescribe medicine to a patient after analyzing numerous diagnostic test results. It can also book the perfect and most cost-optimized itinerary for your upcoming holiday after merely knowing your preferences and activities of interest, while taking into account factors like weather conditions, your fitness level, and who you are traveling with. As you can see, it has, in all practicality, suddenly, replaced an artist, a doctor and a travel agent! This is only the beginning!

AI as the new buzzword

From an outsider's perspective, AI is no longer a differentiator, but a necessary attaché and qualifier to everything: AI-powered phone, AI-powered toaster, AI-enabled vehicles and a prefix to anything and everything you see and hear! If someone is not using this keyword in their names or feature list, they are missing out and will suddenly find themselves at the bottom of the food chain, so to speak! The world's largest companies and governments are putting all their weight behind using, developing, promoting, and sponsoring AI-based solutions in the hardest to imagine problems and scenarios.

This sudden energy surge in all things AI has raised expectations and hope around what the human race can achieve in various facets of life. The world at large is imagining tailored and personalized medical treatment that eliminates long waits for a doctor's appointment. They are also seeking answers to complex, multi-part questions that are difficult for a human to understand and answer due to the limited knowledge one person can have. ChatGPT does not get irritated or bored with your long conversations required to get your problem solved, nor will it get tired or stressed out and start producing wrong results, just as a human might do! It does not need a cup of coffee, bio break or a vacation ever!

Closer look at the current scenario

Let us look more closely and try to make sense of what has been happening around us! First and foremost, let us start by accepting the reality of AI (pun intended). AI is here, it is real and it is here to stay. Secondly, it is definitely and already making our lives easier by many of the applications we touched upon earlier. Moreover, just like technology in general, it is a great asset and time saver.

Take web search for instance. Imagine you want to find 'how old Leonardo was when the classic movie Titanic was released?'. The search engine now interprets the entire question entered by us and provides a pointed answer instead of picking up just the keywords and providing a never-ending list of links, which one must click through one by one to narrow down what one was looking for. Not just that, it elaborates the topic a bit more and provides more supplementing information, links, pictures, suggestions, and more. It is like having a human do the web search for you and then after doing all the heavy lifting, reverting to you with precisely what you needed, in doubly quick time! And to top it all, the accuracy of the answers is near perfect!

Let us turn to some more real and rather challenging scenarios. Let us take an example of a meeting happening at night, which you cannot attend, but your colleagues on the other side of the world are gracious enough to record and share with you. However, you are still required to spend that hour or more going through the recording, sometimes having to rewind and rewatch stuff and listening closely so you understand everything accurately! Not only does it take more time than the duration of the said meeting, but it is also a very tedious and error-prone task!

Enter the AI bot to the rescue! It not only can present a crisp summary and major takeaways of an hour-long meeting, which you can grasp in mere five minutes, but will also explicitly prepare a list of action items and follow-ups, tagged to the respective owner for easy takeaways. Last, but not the least, this effectively results in you, someone who did not spend an hour and did not in fact, attend the meeting, being more efficient and effective than those who spent the hour attending it!

Other side of the story

Enough with the rosy picture! Now, let us look at some grayer scenarios (real or perception). AI has all the goodness of humans, without any shortcomings or demands, so why does one need humans? Is it not a thought-provoking proposition, if not a scary one? Staying away from fear factor and skepticism, let us look at things more closely and objectively.

Let us build further on the meeting scenario we talked about. In the past, in every meeting, we usually would have a designated role of the note taker who would pay attention to not only every word being said, but who is saying it to whom, is it a question or direction or action item; note it down quickly without missing anything while taking notes; and at times even interrupting the speaker for requesting to repeat or explain what they said. At the end, they would rewrite things more concisely, tag each required person manually to the respective minute of the meeting, and share the notes with everyone, with a disclaimer of sorts: *please add anything I might have missed*, to excuse themselves proactively for any possible human errors. Now, the said AI bot not only has taken place of this role, thus taking away the job of the said *note taker*, but it also does its job silently, without intruding the actual proceedings and with minimal possible errors (albeit it still likely flags a disclaimer, something like: *AI-generated content may be inaccurate* to ensure that where something seems odd, the human in the loop is double checking to fill the gap of any inaccuracy). Similarly, AI has become highly efficient and effective at providing you with a crisp **too long; did not read** (**TL; DR**) of a large email or a 100-pager document or book (like the one you are reading now) or a busy PowerPoint presentation, to name a few.

Staying with this example of a virtual or hybrid meeting, previously, at times, one's presentation, communication, and language skills were required to be exemplary, and were tested because a human who is on the other end might have a completely different language understanding or specialization. However, the AI can now interpret many different languages, accents, and dialects, and on the fly, it can also switch to a different one if participants are from a diverse set in this regard! There goes another job: that of a language specialist or interpreter! Also, the said speakers can stop spending time and money on honing those skills. These skills, which were previously essential because they worked in a team with other humans, might not make them effective at their job or help the firm add to the bottom line anymore. So, you might wonder, are those soft skills trainers no longer needed?

We are just warming up with the most obvious and straightforward impact of AI (both the positive and the not-so-positive one) on us. Let us come closer to the life of the intended audience of this book: the people managers.

World of managers

In most companies, the role of a manager is first and foremost to run the business effectively. The part of managing the team effectively is just a 'how' of the job in a nutshell: gone are the days where one used to see layers of leadership hierarchy in place to 'manage' teams. Today, when every company and organization watches every penny being spent, everyone is expected to 'do more with less', and more so, for someone in the role of a manager. It should be noted that in many headcount discussions, managers are often classified as 'overheads' for calculation purposes, as this helps assess the team's bandwidth and estimate the timelines for the work they can take on. From the people management part of their job, a large and most important part of what a manager does, is to write performance reviews for each employee. This activity requires a lot of time, effort, and patience from the manager, which also takes away from the core responsibility of running the business and ensuring the bottom-line for the organization. Its effectiveness comes with all sorts of possible biases: recency bias, personal affinities, and so on. These biases, if not impossible, are very hard to eliminate as humans, and this also means spending a lot of time and effort in anti-bias training for the managers to do their, well, not so core job effectively! To top it all, performance reviews and evaluations result in being too subjective. Everyone wants to work for that super amazing manager and the organization would struggle to scale if only a handful of managers can be considered 'good'!

Enter the AI bot that the reader would be familiar with by now! It can effectively write the almost finished version of a performance review, after going through the self-assessment of the employee, feedback received by peers, email conversations, documents, and other collaterals created by the employee. The manager needs to possibly eyeball it, tweak things here and there, and then could emerge as that superman(ager) for their team as well as for the organization! Managers are happy: they are practical and efficient and are able to focus most energy on the business aspects and things they like doing; employees are happy because they can see their performance is accurately and objectively assessed and the organization is pleased because every manager it has is a superstar people manager and they now possibly need a lot less managers in the overall organization, thus saving them money too because typically managers are expected to cost much higher amounts of money than your average employee!

Next up in the list of typical managerial duties is presenting their vision, roadmaps, list of tasks and updates to leadership. This requires an entirely different set of skills—almost like a salesperson—along with a lot more time and focus, because the stakes are too high to make a mistake. By now, you know that AI can convert your plain English thoughts to mind-bogglingly attractive presentations with crisp stories, studded with pictures and videos to make the narrative easy to receive and engaging! Since we already used up a superhero reference, let us call it becoming the superstar salesman(ager)! So now those 'excellent PowerPoint skills' are no longer a differentiator on your resume: let us strike them out first!

Hopefully, by now, you are getting a picture of how AI is able to silently but swiftly and effectively impact the job of a human in a positive way but also claim a big part of several 'jobs of humans'!

Upcoming effects of AI on the horizon

In this section, we will try to predict what and how AI is expected to affect us in the mid to long-term. We will use a generic set of examples and scenarios as a foundation for the more technical things to come in the later chapters.

AI as an assisting hand

The most apparent, non-intrusive, and most widespread role AI would be playing is that of a helping hand for almost anything we want to do. In this role, AI will be sitting on the sidelines waiting for us to summon it, just like a faithful and trusty friend who knows all intimate details about us, but is someone who has a life and does not disturb us from their end. Let us call it **AIlFred** (on the lines of *Alfred*, the faithful butler for *Batman*), pronounced as *Aisle-Fred*! And we will be its hu-man (a.k.a. *Batman*).

Sample case 1: Money management

Refer to the following prompt:

Human: Hey AIlFred, I got my pay-check today. Can you tell me where I should invest my money?

AIlFred: Certainly, master human! But I think you don't have enough money to make any meaningful investments!

Human (taken aback): What do you mean AIlFred?

AIlFred: I noticed that your expenditure is unusually high compared to how much you earn!

Human (mildly offended): How can you say that? And you are getting too personal!

AIlFred: I am your friend and want the best for you always! You are in your early 30s, but I noticed that in the last month you had to visit the doctor 3 times for stomach-related issues and also had to spend a bunch of money on purchasing medicine. This total spend was roughly 15% of your salary! In my opinion, it is also correlated with the high number of times you ate out at restaurants, a relatively high number in the last month! Not to mention that took up another 15% of your salary!

Human (a bit calmer now): Thanks AIlfred for opening my eyes! I love food! It seems hard to change. What do you suggest?

AIlFred: I can understand! You can start by reducing this by a small portion at time! Instead of visiting a restaurant 4 times, you can do it 3 times in a month, thus, easily cutting the expense down by around 25%! This will also likely spoil your health a lot less and likely cut down your medical expenses by 25% or more. Suddenly you have an extra stash of money you can now invest and grow, that too without changing your lifestyle any significantly!

Human (grateful): Thanks AIlfred! You are a true friend! Please tap me gently in the future if I am exceeding this limit! So where can I invest this money?

AIlFred: Certainly! You don't have to thank me! So, I think with these changes, you will have around 30% of your salary easily available to invest! I see that you are still young, and I think you can take a bit more risk. Let's evaluate the stock market and find the best stocks and mutual funds together which we can consider investing in for the best results in the long term!

<And they lived happily ever after>

Sample case 2: Healthy conversations

Refer to the following prompt:

Human: AIlFred, I want to lose weight, but I am too lazy to go to gym. Can you tell me what I can do?

AIlFred: Certainly, master human! I would say, though, that looking for shortcuts is not a good idea and is not very sustainable!

Human: AIlFred, I asked you for a solution and not a lecture!

AIlFred: Surely! It is my duty as your well-wisher to show you the right direction! And that is surely part of the solution!

Human: Let's get to the point AIlFred!

AIlFred: Master Human sir! You can follow the 80-20 rule. 80% is about diet and habits and 20% about exercise. Many people follow a simple rule of calorie deficit. To achieve that, either you increase your calorie burn or reduce your calorie intake. I realize you are not looking to go the first way, so that means you must reduce your calorie intake, meaning eat less!

Human: AIlfred, why are you so against my happiness? Asking me to stop eating; you know how much I love food!

AIlFred: Not at all, Sir human! Not everyone who praises you is your well-wisher and one who gives you honest feedback is not always your enemy!

Human: I know AIlFred, I am just a bit frustrated!

AIlFred: No problem. So, the good news is that you don't have to sacrifice your love for food in any significant way. Even if you cut down on 10% of your intake and/ or replace it with healthier options or drink more water, you will start your weight loss journey! When you are ready, let's sit down and prepare a plan!

Human: Thanks, AIlfred! You are the best!

AIlFred: Always here for you master human sir!

<And they lived healthily ever after!>

As you can see, just like a close friend, who is with you all the time, you do not have to give much context to get to the point and, the conversation itself is enjoyable; solving the problem at hand is almost a side effect. More importantly, AI in this role is not imposing itself or injecting itself into your life but is practically an extension of your inner monologue, although with the power of knowledge of the wide world! Occasionally, if you want it to, this well-wisher of yours will notice something unusual about you and might proactively warn or suggest you take a closer look: say an unusually irritating tone, a raised heartbeat, an inconsistent sleep pattern or an abnormal change in your routine!

For a manager, an example scenario could be consulting **AIlfred** to interpret an email, an interaction with a team member, or a sequence of events over the last few days when you have a doubt or want a second opinion on what you are thinking.

This role of AI is possibly the most complementary and pleasant for us to adapt to and likely will see a surge in the coming times. It can make humans appear as superstars and experts at their job, and save precious time from mundane tasks, thus enabling them to take on more higher-level stuff, building on the work of AI. On the flip side, where previously we might have gone to say, a finance or nutrition specialist, we end up getting the help from our AI friend itself, thus making the demand and job for either of those professionals significantly reduced, if not wholly taken over on paper at least! As another side effect, this might shape the education system, courses and specializations offered in the institutes away from these kinds of areas on paper at least! The effects can seep in many other ways as well in the world as we know it.

AI as a reviewer

In this role, AI will be like an 'oracle' or 'test suite' or a 'bouncing board' for the work of a human. You prepared a recipe, or have an idea or proposal, or you prepared an important presentation, and you want to make sure that it is up to the mark and will land the impact you were going for. Let us take a few examples to drive this home.

Many big movie houses are doubling down on doing 'test screening' of their new movies with a limited, **nondisclosure agreement** (**NDA**) signed or an 'insider' audience before they release it. They do it to know how the real audience will react, and have an opportunity to make any changes before the final cut. However, this approach has a couple of drawbacks: one is the very likely possibility of spoilers going out, and secondly, the handpicked audience is not necessarily a fair representation of the actual audience and also likely will be biased in some way (say because they are from film fraternity, they likely might cringe on anything which is too outside of movies which sell at the box office). If you imagine an AI in its place, you can address both these issues and also possibly tune the 'bias' to be that of your target audience demographic!

Let us take another example. You have prepared a sales pitch, and you want to see the reaction to it from a real client before you present it to the actual client, since a lot is at stake, and do not want to leave any room for failure! Instead, you can engage AI, provide few key details about your client and instruct it to play the role of that client. Then present the pitch with all your charm and vigor, without the fear of failure, and get the exact feedback you might have received from the real client, but a few hours earlier. Kind of like you have the superpower of time travel to travel to the future and back!

Taking one more example might be helpful. Let us say you are a manager, and you have an upcoming hard conversation with one of your team members and are worried about the possibility of it going wrong. You do want to land the message but do not want to risk upsetting the motivation or productivity of the said team member. In this scenario, AI can easily play the role of that one teammate for a while, and you can really see how the conversation might go. You can tweak things till you get it right before the prime time!

To summarize, in this role, AI will likely emerge as the elder brother or sister, a trusted mentor, or an advanced self-help ecosystem or guide! This has the potential to change or dethrone many of the professional streams, like coaching and mentorship professions. Or those who are into training humans for skills that might now become redundant or impractical! On paper at least! Instead, the skills people will try to learn and develop are to tune or prompt the AI to position it for the best results possible, mimicking the job of an actual human doing the review of their work.

AI in the driver's seat

In this role, AI is calling the shots, a Steven SpAIlberg if you will! In a nutshell, this represents cases where a human is not required in the loop. Talking about drivers, the first example that comes to mind is of self-driving cars, fully automated homes, or an AI taking up a creative role all by itself, such as a renowned painter like *Leonardo da Vinci* or a celebrated author like *Shakespeare*!

This has recently started happening in parts and is in a nascent phase where a human is expected to try a few different 'prompts' to get the AI to generate the required text, image, voice, or video outcome or take an action. This is still a trial-and-error method, and a more reverse engineering approach; where one tries to find what exactly they should ask and tell the AI to get it to do the best possible outcome. Moreover, the generated content is far from perfect; it is often inconsistent or incoherent. But with the army of software and hardware engineers, data scientists and creators relentlessly working on it as we speak, this aspect is likely to get its kinks ironed out in a not-so-distant future.

Once AI reaches that state, then it will likely start being deployed to do many of the jobs of a human, which are traditionally considered to be only possible by humans, as stated earlier. For example, those which are more on the 'creative' side of the world, which most of the jobs in practice are. Most jobs humans do are part science, but a lot of art. Even those that are seemingly far removed from a 'creative' job—such as programming (a computer)—are, in fact, considered an art: the art of making the best use of programming language constructs to get the computer to do things that were not done before, thereby contributing to the advancement of software technology.

In the context of people management, an extreme case of this category might be about where companies offload most of the 'management' work, such as assessing people's performance, planning and driving projects or doing 1:1s with the team members. Hence, managers are primarily expected to play the role of an expert individual contributor and bring real business impact and value instead of being just a 'layer' in the organizational hierarchy!

This particular role of AI is most likely the one that will be super disruptive to how we live and work, as well as the cause of many ongoing and upcoming discussions and fears of AI taking away our jobs! From a human's point of view, this also might mean that a whole set of skills, like learning tools like PowerPoint expertise, are neither required nor special enough to be needed for employment. It is probably time to think of evolving skills that one learns, which is necessary to decide how and where to deploy AI effectively in a fire and forget mode. It is an exciting time to leave the mundane behind and concentrate on more significant and more innovative things.

Ethical considerations of AI

This is an incredibly involved, sensitive, and debated topic, and the book does not attempt to be comprehensive about it. We will try to look at this dimension a bit closely with the intention of creating awareness of this side of working with AI with some examples. To get this aspect right, we recommend that you consult an expert and read the fine print of any technology you might use, build, or build on.

Temptation to cross that imaginary line

Just like any other tool or technology, AI brings a whole lot of morally and ethically gray areas with it. For instance, in the not-too-distant past, with the advent of advanced image and video 'filters' on smartphone cameras, most people posted pictures that looked nothing like what they looked like in real life. This brought them a lot more views and, in turn, made them richer and more popular. Should that be considered morally or ethically acceptable?

Similarly, in music, 'auto-tune' can potentially make an ordinary singer sound like a fantastic rockstar, and thus increase their popularity, social and economic status. But the world is, of course, divided on whether this is acceptable versus personal choice or blatant cheating. Similar conversations can be had for cosmetic surgery in glamour and visual arts!

Now that we understand why these usages of technology have been a debatable ethical practice even before this wave of AI, let us look at what the new AI wave brings!

Difficulty in spotting AI-generated content

With the technologists chipping away quickly at the goal of making AI more and more performant and invisible in its work, it is getting next to impossible to detect if AI has been used for something or not, which being the whole point of it being close to being human-like. For instance, if you see a video showcasing someone's excellent acrobatic skills, you will instantly applaud the awe-inspiring gymnast in them, without knowing if this is AI-generated or at the minimum, AI-enhanced. Now that one knows that this is possible through AI, we start disbelieving anything that comes up until it is proven that it is real: the classic 'innocent until guilty' or 'guilty until innocent' paradigm!

The harder it becomes to spot the difference between original and AI-generated work or content, the harder it becomes to not use or spot it!

Bending the rules

In many cases, even if you are not directly using AI to improve or fix your work, one might use unauthorized data or content to train or fine-tune AI, thus getting an unfair advantage without directly crossing the ethical line. Or even using jailbreak or the gaps of hallucination in AI to force it to possibly reveal internal or protected information and gain an upper hand! It is important to know that sooner or later, laws get tightened, and the law catches up with these loopholes or gray areas; thus, it is advisable to build the foundation itself in an ethical way from the start.

Now that we have laid ground regarding ethics and integrity about the use of AI, let us look at some dimensions to think about when embracing AI or the AI-enabled world itself!

Responsible AI

This is a crucial consideration, especially if you are providing AI as a service or platform, wherein you do not have direct control over how AI-generated work comes out, because it is unpredictable and dynamic, and you cannot test all possible cases in advance, unlike traditional software engineering-based products and technologies. So, what this aspect effectively means is one should add safeguards as much as possible for proactively ensuring the AI is acting 'responsibly' and also have a way to reactively and quickly plug any holes that ended up surfacing in real-world scenarios. This includes covering for offensive language or narratives, politically or demographically sensitive topics, outcomes, and so on. For example, for a product offering chat-based web search, this means taking accountability of, and keeping a tab on age-inappropriate, non-factual or confidential content leaking to the user.

Plagiarism

As we discussed in some of the examples earlier, it is becoming super convenient to project AI-generated work/content as one's original work, as well as harder for the receiver to catch or claim that it is not original. Added to the fact that AI now always generates unique and 'original' content, in reality, no one can claim that the user has copied someone else's work. Thus, this shifts the responsibility solely to the user of AI to ensure that they do not use AI in places where they are showcasing something as their own authentic work, just like the writing of this book.

One obvious example of this kind of unethical practice is someone using AI in technical interviews where the intent is to evaluate the skills and experience of the human candidate giving an interview. Thus, clearly in this case, the usage of AI-generated work is not a fair representation of their capability for which they will be hired and paid for! While humans and interviewing tools are quickly becoming more and more intelligent to spot such malpractice, the candidate themselves need to take accountability of staying authentic. In a traditional sense, this is effectively the same as cheating in classroom exams, where the teacher or invigilator is not always able to spot those, but that does not mean one is clear to use the malpractice!

Conclusion

In this chapter, we took stock of the breadth and landscape on the ground in the age of AI to understand at a high-level how AI is coming into our lives and the kind of impact and benefits it is having. We also probed with an objective view, the fear of it taking away our jobs, or making us incompetent or redundant. Lastly, we not only addressed the technical aspects of AI but also examined the social, legal, and ethical implications associated with building and using AI systems. While the grapevine might be that humans are quickly going to become redundant or out of jobs, we also touched on how humans have the advantage and opportunity to evolve to the next stage and turn this seeming bane to a boon by effectively leveraging AI for the right kind of stuff. By doing so, humans move on to the next set of human tasks!

In the next and concluding chapter of this section, we will try to build a framework and thought process for finding applications and impacts of AI in one's specific field of work or domain. We will continue to keep it somewhat generic but with a closer eye on the managers working in the field of software and technology.

Join our Discord space

Join our Discord workspace for latest updates, offers, tech happenings around the world, new releases, and sessions with the authors:

https://discord.bpbonline.com

CHAPTER 2
Applications of AI in Your Domain

Introduction

This is the second of the two chapters on the topic of embracing the power of AI. In this chapter, we will build on the groundwork and background set in the previous chapter and, using that, find ways to think about AI's role in a specific domain. This chapter continues to be for a generic audience with a hint of focus on the software engineering and people management domain. As before, throughout the narrative, the book attempts to stay balanced, objective, and rational in the picture being painted.

Structure

This chapter covers the following topics:

- AI tools for team productivity
- Domain-specific AI tools
- Exploring further possible applications of AI
- Keeping up with the happenings in the AI space

Objectives

By the end of this chapter, we will have built another layer in the foundation for the rest of the book, that is, understanding AI applications in software engineering and management. We will look at some practically possible examples of this, but also try to give the reader some food for thought regarding how to think about the possible addition of AI, even if your world is slightly different.

AI tools for team productivity

Productivity-related use cases are possibly the easiest win-win scenarios for managers when it comes to applying AI. Let us dissect it now.

Business reality

Business outcomes are the centerpiece of any organization; typically, revenue, profit, and **return on investment (ROI)** are the obvious targets to achieve. As a manager, these are generally your primary accountabilities, and you can play an essential part in some or all of these. Think of this as, while the 'what' that your team needs to do and deliver will be largely driven top-down or by business, deciding the 'how' for your team is something you, as the manager, typically have a larger control over and are empowered to do. The easiest one you can contribute to without changing the nature of your business is the ROI, by finding ways to maximize your team's output. If your team's productivity is improved by just 20%, it is like having a team of 12 members at the cost of 10! Not just that, other benefits of using these tools include a boost to the team's energy and morale because they are doing fewer repetitive and monotonous tasks. On top of that, as part of their regular job, they are now learning new skills and keeping themselves relevant in the AI paradigm by using and learning AI! As a manager—and for the organization as a whole— this also helps reduce churn and attrition, since employees now look forward to coming to work. They get to be part of exciting new AI-driven initiatives without feeling left out, all while continuing to apply the skills and experience they have built over the years in their respective domains. With this background, let us now look at a few different kinds of tools you can use in software engineering to improve productivity. It is worth noting that many of these currently exist or are soon to become possibilities, judging by the early signs!

AI in the context of coding

This is when AI anticipates what you might need in the context you are in, as well as upon your prompt, provides you with an almost solved answer. As an example of this, let us say one is in the 'coding' context with an **integrated development environment** (**IDE**), that is, a semantics-aware text editing tool.

Various possible coding scenarios

The most probable 'context' of being in coding is obviously writing new code, modifying existing code, or adding comments to improve readability. The other, but slightly less likely context, is that you are trying to 'read' the code, that is, browsing the code to understand the calling chain or the flow. These days, we have many AI tools or plugins that are integrated deeply into the IDE, and thus, can provide you with specific help in your context. In this scenario, such an AI helper can give you a way to prompt it, such as 'add functionality in this class for exposing the state property'. The AI tool can, in place, write code for you that will semantically and syntactically be accurate and do the job that this code is supposed to do. Moreover, without you putting in any effort, it will match the coding style and convention of the existing code! All you need to do now is 'accept' the suggested code, eyeball it quickly to ensure everything is in order, tweak anything you prefer and then save the code and move on to compilation and validation which should be almost a formality now with the AI-generated code which is mostly syntactically and semantically correct from the start.

Magic of AI as a time saver

Let us look at the previous scenario closely. Without AI, this is how the steps might have been:

1. Write the skeleton code.

2. Implement the first cut of the said functionality.

3. Run through multiple rinse-repeat cycles of compilation-testing-fixing till you get it right.

4. Worry about corner cases and implement some from what you can think of.

5. Skim through the existing code's coding convention and style and update your code to match it.

And so on.

But with AI, the steps would be as follows:

1. Describe what the code needs to do via prompting the AI tool, and let it generate the proposal of the code.

2. Eyeball the AI-generated code and 'accept' the changes after any minor tweaks.

3. Compile and sanity check everything is fine.

Purely in terms of time taken, it would easily save you 70-80% of time. Moreover, it will provide additional confidence that the code will compile successfully on the first attempt and be free from any human errors or non-obvious nasty bugs that might show up late in the development cycle or, worse, in the field! With the right prompts and training, the AI tool can also help ensure other non-functional requirements, such as security, privacy, or scale-related considerations, by choosing the right constructs when multiple options are available. Moreover, in this bargain, the developer will complete their tasks much sooner! This extra time, can be used in taking on more work, new learning, or sharing knowledge, fun activities, or taking a well-deserved break to get recharged, which further improves one's productivity!

A similar journey can also be undertaken if one is looking to refactor existing code, add more comments, fix the style to make the code easier to understand, browse the code to learn the overall high-level flow, or figure out the best way to fix a bug at hand.

AI in the context of quality assurance

Another phase of the end-to-end software lifecycle is testing and quality assurance, where AI can more naturally and effectively wield its magic.

Generating new tests at the click of a button

Many AI tools integrated into the IDE can now write or update unit test cases with the click of a button. This would have previously taken even more time than writing the actual code one is trying to test. One must consider and implement all possible test scenarios that the code is expected to handle in production. The developer might have missed many key or corner scenarios since they are limited by their knowledge and context. IDE-integrated AI tools can now (or in the near future) analyze the code, bring in the 'wisdom' of any test cases ever written in the world, including the codebase of this product, to come up with the most optimum and efficient set of test code to provide coverage of all scenarios, line and branch coverage and so on.

Quality over quantity by optimizing testing

Staying in the context of software testing, another challenge is how much testing is enough for a given code change, a new module or a new piece of code. The balance is between the time it takes to declare the code change as good-to-go and ensuring that everything that needs to be working has been tested. Generally, many build pipelines have a fixed set of tests based on the exit criteria. Over a period of time, as the code evolves, more and more test cases keep getting added, making the test suites bulkier and with longer and longer run times. Not just that, over a period, people will not remember which test cases are testing which scenario. However, we cannot exclude any test from the list of tests because the developer is too afraid to take a chance of missing a test and end up breaking production. Moreover, the tools and pipelines might also not have a way of excluding tests for each code change.

Enter the intelligence and learnability of AI: it can be trained on that software product's build pipeline. It can then help with the test 'selection' logic of picking the minimum number of unique test cases out of the pile to be executed to ensure coverage of the significant functionality relevant to the given code change. Hence, this helps make the developer and the organization much more agile when taking code to production. Moreover, further building on this, the team can, over a period, identify and get rid of stale or redundant tests in their system: those that were never picked by the test selection logic and/or are covering scenarios that overlap with other faster and better test cases.

AI in the context of software architecture and design

In software engineering, architecture and design are crucial aspects. They must be based on the product or solution's requirements and be thoroughly documented. This is important to ensure that the engineer has thought through sufficient high-level technical details before starting to code or making code changes. This is also important for others in the team to be able to know about it, provide input, and drive it.

Requirements for a large code base

During the activity of coming up with a design and architecture, one needs to ensure a few things:

- Seamless integration with the existing system components.

- Choosing the best possible pieces of tech and tools for the given functional and non-functional requirements.

- Anticipating future requirements and making it possible to incorporate them with minimal effort if/when they come.

However, the engineer needs to do some additional things, such as the following, in order to be effective and efficient when a large code base is involved:

- Learn the overall product's architecture, or at the minimum, the neighboring components, sufficiently well.

- Become an expert on the various available options, technical choices for achieving the requirements, and real experience of their pros and cons in practice.

- Spend some time doing prototyping and feasibility testing to validate one's own hypotheses and fill the gap of practical knowledge of the given problem and solution tried.

Magic of AI to the fore

AI, especially **generative AI (GenAI)/large language models (LLMs)**, on the other hand, have 'learned' from pretty much all the designs ever built anywhere in the world, all the possible applications of any technology or data structures, and their real pros and cons when they were deployed in production. Hence, using an AI in this case, makes the human engineer do a job almost equivalent to the most experienced and versatile engineer possible, without having to spend time to learn, build experience, or trial-and-error!

AI for repetitive work

In any profession, especially software engineering, a significant percentage of one's time is spent on repetitive or apparent repetitive work. Let us see what AI can do here. We take an example of 'support' to drive the point home.

Automation as a tried and tested practice

Traditional practice has always been to 'automate' these repetitive-looking tasks. However, automation requires a lot of human time to build, test, and deploy. It is also hard to keep current as time passes and things change. LLMs and AI agent-like tools are ideal to bring in for this. They not only go beyond traditional automation with far less human investment to set up, but they are also intelligent, doing more than just what humans could have thought of while building them. This frees up a significant amount of time for the developer and the team, and at the same time, by using AI, they deliver more quantity of work with better quality. Lastly, humans are not designed to excel at doing the same thing repeatedly. So, this increases their overall productivity because now they are always doing something they have never done (repetitive things offloaded to AI).

Case study for why AI fits support like a glove

Some of the good use cases of the above narrative are handling production issues (also known as, **live site** or **on-call**). These issues generally have a lot of similarities to each other or follow some pattern and mostly need a bunch of well-tried steps to mitigate those issues. Moreover, AI can gather information from multiple sources for example, customer issues, service health, emails, chats and so on and correlate them super quickly and effectively to do a much better and faster job of mitigating the issue. Some of the other advantages AI brings here are:

- Identifying duplicate or related issues.
- Send out crisp and relevant communications to both internal and external stakeholders.
- While doing this, also learn from this 'experience' for future.

A human trained over many years on a loop over the same context might improve to a good extent but for sure cannot come close to the speed, effectiveness, completeness, and finesse of a super-intelligent LLM-based application. This also means that as an individual and as a team, we can tackle a much higher volume of issues because now each issue takes, say, 90% less time as well as human effort than before! Not to mention, this accelerated speed can improve the **service level agreements** (**SLAs**) significantly since no time is being wasted in making things wait, endless analysis, or simply a context switch.

Taking a step further with AI

Another dimension of handling support is frontline support (also known as **customer support**). AI bots have already been acting as frontline support. They can talk to a customer when a customer contacts the support channel. In a different scenario, it can be the first responder of a support ticket filed and do most of the mundane or obvious analysis to weed out well-known issues or extract crisp and important information to help with the response and resolution without spending even a second of human time.

This can also increase the speed and agility of resolving customer issues. Additionally, it will significantly boost customer satisfaction because AI can quickly gather all the context of the customer and the problem, and its conversation will feel like talking to someone familiar, empathetic, and knowledgeable.

Most customer support platforms have a lot of drawbacks, such as:

- Long wait times to get someone to connect with.
- A lot of questions, answers, and explanations to set the context before the problem can be resolved.
- Frustration of starting from scratch each time a call gets disconnected, or a ticket gets closed, and so on.

If AI is configured, trained, and deployed properly in such cases for fronting customer issues, the organization can potentially ace the support game both in terms of quality and volume.

Domain-specific AI tools

We talked about many actual or conceptual tools and applications of AI in the domain of software engineering. Taking a cue from there, let us see how we can find ways to learn about AI tools and applications in any other domain. Moreover, as a manager, you would be expected to have a pulse on people in your team and the execution and business outcome on the ground. AI can be used in achieving some of this as well.

Here is an opportunity to connect those two in this context. In the next few pages, we will see 'how' to do it.

AI as a helping hand

In essence, one of the manager's important responsibilities to their team is to make sure the skills and aspirations of each of the team members align primarily with the work they are asked to do. People typically join an organization and a team because they are passionate about the domain, the mission, and the problems the organization is trying to solve. They also join because of their technical expertise and the skills they have studied or built experience with. However, in real-world scenarios, the work on the ground is always a mix of the 'core' as well as the supplementing work around it.

Helping hand example 1

Let us take a carpenter as an example. They are skilled and experienced in the art of carving wood and connecting many pieces together to create really useful and beautiful constructs. They typically love designing and imagining new furniture and providing insights and suggestions to anyone about the best designs or materials they should use for their home or office.

However, the end-to-end work of getting the furniture built has many other tasks too, which the carpenter must take up: such as buying and transporting material from a shop and going door to door if something is not available in one of them. They might also need to call up and coordinate with the customer about the date and time of doing the work, negotiating and having payment-related discussions, answering calls, and having conversations about many non-technical aspects —these are a necessary evil, so to speak, and assisting tasks for the core carpentry work!

To tackle this, many of the carpenters would have an assistant or two who are typically apprentices but not really experienced with the craft. The carpenter would find it much easier to explain the tasks to them as well as delegate, while they can focus on the more 'evolved' part of the work and the ones they love doing. The assistant, in turn, has a great opportunity to not just be useful but also earn their living. Additionally, by being in the close vicinity of the master carpenter, they learn about the art of carpentry itself over time. This can also result in them gradually being able to offload more and more from the carpenter's plate, even some of the previously considered complex tasks. The carpenter, in turn, can now take on more projects in a similar or shorter time than before. This will help them make more money and enable them to live a more fulfilled and happy life as well, since they are largely doing what they love, as well as bringing the flexibility to give more time for themselves and their family.

Helping hand example 2

Closer to the world of organizations and managers, there could be many scenarios where a helping hand can make them more effective and efficient, such as:

- Preparing full or part of a presentation to save human effort in hand-crafting impactful visuals or narratives.

- Rewriting emails in a much better or more concise manner, keeping the essence, message, and tone.

- Summarizing a long email thread into a two minute quick TL; DR.

- Suggesting the best timeslot for a meeting given the audience and agenda, taking into account the amount and nature of the 'load' of your overall day and week.

AI can easily take on the role of the human assistant in many such cases.

As a manager in your own domain, you must find essential but peripheral tasks that your team members do not find particularly enjoyable. Gradually, move the line towards AI by training it on an ongoing basis, and hence eliminate human involvement by taking up even more aspects of semi-human tasks. Once you look deeper and look around, you will likely find an AI tool or two for your use case(s).

AI as the reviewer

The other role a manager typically plays is to review the work of their team members before it goes out to the world. Alternatively, they use a more senior person in the team to do this, with the work of other junior team members. Both ways, 'reviewing'/ 'overseeing' the work of others is an essential job the manager needs to get done. Clearly, this can make them the bottleneck for their team's impact and delivery. However, they must do it because they are accountable for their team's work towards the rest of the organization and customers.

Reviewer example 1

With this backdrop, let us take the example of a head chef of a reputed hotel. A head chef is responsible for the preparation of cuisine on a large-scale, typically with the help of a team that would be doing a major part of the heavy lifting and work in the kitchen. The head chef would start by explaining the overall spread they need to prepare for the time of the day, explain the recipes, and then leave them to do their work of preparing the food. They will then decide the 'checkpoints' of when and how they will review the progress and preparation of each dish and go about visually inspecting or tasting a sample of the overall fleet of work, and provide inputs or directions. They might also taste or sample from the fully prepared cuisine at the end, too, before the food makes it to the customers.

Clearly, the manager (head chef) has a specialized job to do in order for the kitchen army to scale. Even if they hire a few more sub-head chefs to delegate this, maintaining quality and speed is still a challenge.

In the context of AI tools, this clearly is a job for a fine-tuned AI tool that can do the reviewer's job 90-100% depending upon the criticality of each task and the maturity of the tool or model it is built on. Benefit-wise, this approach can make the quality of the end outcome even more uniform, and the manager and the organization can scale to do a lot more output without compromising quality.

Reviewer example 2

Another use case of such a thing could be in the education sector. When a teacher prepares a question paper, they might want to assess and tune its effectiveness in evaluating the best students. At times, they also want to assess and tune the exam paper's degree of complexity for the students. However, they fear the danger of leaking the test paper if they want to get a second opinion, so they have to rely on their own point of view.

Imagine having a virtual student (or a diversified group of students) who can take this test first. This will enable the teacher to quickly analyze both these aspects with real feedback to assess and tweak accordingly. They can then take the exam paper with the utmost confidence to the real students for the actual exam. Similarly, if they want to ensure that their exam paper is not very similar to the previous 3 years' papers, they can use the help of AI to review their paper, evaluate the 'similarity quotient' with those, and help tweak or move forward!

AI in the driver's seat

Now, this can be rather nerve-wracking, especially for a manager, and more so for the team members to learn that it is not their manager, a human, but an AI that is in the driver's seat and deciding their fate! This is much less melodramatic than that, though. Let us see how.

Driver's seat example 1

As before, let us deep-dive into this with an example. Everyone in the team generally comes to work with the intention and hope of doing their core tasks. Commute is an essential but not a core part of what the employees are expected to do. So, every day, depending upon how far each of them stays from the office, they take a different amount of time away from work or from home to drive to work.

Enter the AI in the driver's seat (literally), who now drives you to work. All of a sudden, this could enable the employees to utilize the commute time to complete part of their work or preparation or even do any personal work. As you can see, by offloading a task completely to AI, the human would have gained valuable time back and we know time is money too! Not just that, a human driver can quickly lose focus and make errors on the road, resulting in fatality or disruption in their routine for the short or long-term, especially if their mind is occupied with work or personal life-related things or in a stressful situation and that can compound this misery. This is no longer a challenge with AI in the driver's seat. What is more, 'being a skilled driver' is no longer a job requirement for the employee. Thus, your reach as an employer suddenly becomes much more extensive. Now you can hire that superstar of your domain who was not in the frame because they are not a good driver or are not interested in doing that daily!

If you look deeper as a manager, you will see tasks you are either doing for your team or having your team do that can be completely offloaded to AI and 'fire and forget' in many cases. Thus, this category of AI use case is ideal!

Driver's seat example 2

Another example of this can be easily thought of in a teaching scenario. A teacher is expected to go through and evaluate 10s or 100s of answer sheets every few months, depending on the cadence of term exams in their class. This is easily a task that can be handled independently by an advanced AI of the new era. It would not only evaluate objective or multiple-choice questions but could now venture into subjective or literature questions, which only a human teacher could previously tackle. The human teacher can now be more stress-free and have more time on their hand to possibly spend on more learning and betterment of the students!

Exploring further possible applications of AI

This section tries to build a framework and mindset of looking beyond what is there to what is possible and how to go about finding not-so-obvious use cases in pretty much any field you work in. As a manager, this will also help you make a larger impact on the organization by bringing in more value proactively! Not to mention that this will help you, the team, and the organization stay relevant and ahead of the curve by keeping up with the advancements in your specific domain and the world at large!

Necessity as the mother of invention in the AI space

This tried, tested, and somewhat cliché adage is one of the best ways to know what you do not know. Let us look at a few ways to go about it.

Learning the necessity

As a manager, putting yourself in the team member's shoes and experiencing things on the ground yourself is a good idea. This will help you stay hands-on and rooted in ground reality and automatically equip you with ideas regarding things that seem like overhead or are being done inefficiently. This will motivate you to think about newer and better ways to do things. As a seasoned manager, you will likely start by asking, *are there others doing it in a better way already?* That will push you to learn from others and find any solutions that already exist in the wild!

Innovating on others' necessities

It is also a good idea sometimes to discuss and learn from other managers in the community, both within and outside the organization. If you want to push even further, you can, in fact, 'survey' the other managers around you or in a larger demographic to learn about their necessities and pain points. Additionally, know if they are using AI in any other creative way or have thoughts on painful tasks that they do, that they wish they could get off their plates. Someone else's pain/ necessity could be an opportunity for invention for you to explore better ways of doing those things, including the use of AI.

Decoupling the person from the role

The other kind of opportunities to innovate and introduce AI for a manager can originate from things that you believe your team members associate with you as the person, as opposed to looking at objectively as part of the role of a manager. If you introduce AI to take on some of those, the team members would be able to differentiate the 'role' from the 'person' behind the role. This will make them see the 'objective' nature of those aspects and help them be more at peace and accepting of those actions or directions.

Some of the examples of these aspects could be as follows:

- Having an AI provide an objective summary of the team members' work over the semester for performance review purposes. This might be an extreme example but a feasible one, and might make the performance review hugely comprehensive and objective.

- Using AI to prepare the draft version of the 'action plan' for the team based on an employee survey, instead of providing your own interpretation of the results, which might be biased.

- Things like collecting feedback or doing sprint retrospectives could be partly or completely driven by AI, ensuring unarguable anonymity for the participants and thus paving the way for more objective and factual inputs from them.

Conventions are inventions in the space of AI

With all the freed-up time and new energy brought on by small or large extents of AI usage, this will likely enable you as the manager to attend more seminars and conventions in your domain and learn not just about what is going on but what people are buzzing about or seeing on the horizon!

Going back to being a learner

Getting out of the grounded and 'real' set of situations and venturing into the world of ideas and possibilities could help awaken your creative brain to its fullest and give you the mental space to imagine the possibilities of what you can experiment with, including ways to utilize the capabilities of AI for your specific domain. You also get to earn the awe and respect of your team members and your leadership chain by bringing new cutting-edge ideas and thoughts, and, thus, things they are unaware of or have not thought of. They do not say this for nothing: 'knowledge is power'!

Idea generation and hackathon sessions

In addition to listening to and learning from other experts' views via seminars, you, as a manager, can also drive and facilitate such sessions and forums. You can think of driving fireside chats, hackathons, idea generation sessions, and so on. This can bring multiple brains together to generate possibilities, proofs of concepts, proposals, or data for building cases of making things better via AI, amongst other things.

Keeping up with the happenings in the AI space

All managers who want to evolve and grow and keep themselves relevant and respected should make learning their lifelong objective.

Your role may be getting in your way

Yes, indeed, let us see how! As a manager, you are given a role where you are expected to provide directions to others who are less skilled or less experienced than you. Hence, it is super easy to get into a mindset that you know-it-all and do not have significantly more left to learn about your domain, as well as things like soft skills, managerial skills, or AI. The team members will be following you and your direction diligently. However, it does not always mean that

that is because you are the expert, but many times because they do not know better or they have no choice because they report to you!

Hence, many folks in managerial roles very soon get into a stagnant and self-fulfilling satisfaction stage with the inclination to keep the status quo. The desire to learn and evolve can quickly diminish because of a lack of incentive to do so. One might get a wake-up jolt one fine day out of the blue, and if that happens, you will be in a challenging situation! It is tough to change one's habits built over many years and come out of this inertia and start 'learning' it might be too late by that time anyway!

What you can do

The objective here is to find ways to keep up with the latest developments as well as advancements in AI in and around your domain. In the modern world, as soon as even an iota of an idea or development happens, numerous tutorials, trainings, and certifications present themselves. Given these easy-to-consume media, one could easily take time out for learning and leveraging them. Many companies also incentivize their employees to have a learning mindset by having an education or learning budget.

Conclusion

In this chapter, we took a closer look at the opportunities of introducing and leveraging AI in various aspects, especially in a team working on software development. The potential uses of AI that we have learned are vast. They are only limited by one's creativity and mindset when imagining the possibilities and capabilities of what AI can do. We also learned that from an outsider's perspective, there might be fear and uncertainty about introducing AI into their lives, especially about making themselves redundant as humans. However, AI has the potential to help make human lives better and evolve.

The next three chapters will take the reader one more step closer to their AI journey by learning more about the team members they are leading. We will tackle this by segmenting the team members into three broad personas, and the next chapter will cover one of those personas in detail.

Join our Discord space

Join our Discord workspace for latest updates, offers, tech happenings around the world, new releases, and sessions with the authors:

https://discord.bpbonline.com

CHAPTER 3
Type A, the Wide-eyed Ones

Introduction

In this section, we will try to learn more about the different types of personas a manager might have in their team when it comes to AI orientation. The process of doing this will help us understand the composition of our specific team better. Moreover, it will help us decide our overall planning and strategy in a much more realistic, tailored, and grounded way.

The book divides them into three broad categories, and the next three chapters dive deeper into each of them, respectively. In practice, a person will not strictly belong to one of these three categories but will likely have a relatively closer match to one of the three as compared to the other two. Everyone is unique, and the book does not attempt to stereotype or typecast individuals. What we instead try to do is, in the context of AI, adopt a growth mindset and strive to understand where they are coming from, enabling the right kind of dialogue and input as a manager to inform the next steps for the team. We will reserve the later chapters for solutions around this, but will try to stick to learning more about these personas in the respective chapter dedicated to each of them.

In this chapter, we look at the first one. These are the folks who are like the proverbial clean slate or mold of clay from an AI knowledge and experience perspective, and thus are still in the process of formation. Typically, they are very curious about AI and are eager to learn.

Structure

This chapter covers the following topics:

- Identifying and defining this persona
- Learning more by having a dialogue with them
- Managing their expectations
- Educating them on tools and use cases of AI

Objectives

In this chapter, we will strive to gain a clear understanding of how the first type of persona in your team thinks, what works for them, and what does not, as well as the strategy for guiding them along the AI journey in the most effective and organic way. This will lead us to find ways to help move them to form more stable and objective points of view from the volatile state they start from.

Identifying and defining this persona

The title of this chapter likely reveals a great deal about the persona. Let us examine this persona more closely and identify a few key characteristics. The team members in this segment are likely to include, but not be limited to, early-career employees, who are most likely to be highly impressionable.

At the extreme ends of the spectrum

The personnel in this category often appear to change their opinions frequently as new information or news emerges. On a given day, they would appear to be working in one of two modes: either as an AI believer or an AI skeptic. On the onset, they typically possess polarized but volatile opinions that keep swaying based on what they hear or are being told by folks around.

On the one hand, when they are in a pro-AI mode, they would likely want to find problems with the AI solution in anything they do or see around them. On the other extreme, they might be terrified and paranoid about the wave of AI, worrying that it will take away their jobs or portray AI in a way similar to the evil robot version most sci-fi movies depict.

Skeptic about authority

They are typically apprehensive about taking things at face value, especially when coming from people in authority, and instead try to quickly confirm or align with things their colleagues or those with similar experience levels are saying.

Untouched by the real AI

Another way to understand this person is that they typically have not had deep experience with either the problems that AI attempts to solve or have not been part of the development of AI technologies and solutions. Rather, they have been shaped by secondary or tertiary knowledge regarding AI.

Safety in conformance

In addition, for them, the source of information and truth is typically what their colleagues and equals are saying and thinking, as well as the influencers they follow; they believe these influencers are more credible and feel safer in aligning with the currently popular opinion rather than standing out by saying something contrary.

Group mentality

Another trait or symptom of this persona is that they exhibit a group mentality. An easy way to spot this is that many of them use very similar terminology, language, or phrases. They would be very open to sharing anything they heard or said to someone amongst themselves. If you spoke to one of them in a one-on-one setting, and then if you happen to talk to another person on the team, you will realize that they are also up-to-date on that conversation and might cite it directly or indirectly.

Moreover, in a group setting, if you ask a question or open up for questions, you as the manager are unlikely to see anyone of this persona stepping up into the limelight. On the contrary, they are likely to be very forthcoming and even pushy in one-on-one conversations because they hold very strong, black-and-white views on all things AI, but they do not want to stand out in the group.

Learning more by having a dialogue with them

As a manager, in most scenarios and situations, the recommended first step is to listen and learn; we call it your 'tell me more' move!

Let us divide it into looking at 'what', 'why', and 'how'. Having a heart-to-heart conversation and lending a listening ear as a manager also has a positive side effect of building trust and close relationships with the individual, which can further help with other aspects, not just the AI-related conversation and planning.

Learning 'what' they know

In this era of social media and numerous platforms, various buzzwords and perceptions surround nearly everything, and AI is no exception. It is almost impossible to differentiate facts from opinions, real information from rumors, and correlation from conjecture.

Hence, as a manager, it is crucial to understand what team members of this persona know about AI and its capabilities. Their 'knowledge' and opinion will likely be a combination of various sources, including hearsay, fact and fiction, word-of-mouth, and their interpretation of what was told, among others. As explained earlier, they are unlikely to have a substantial proportion of their own first-hand knowledge and experiences of AI forming their knowledge base.

As part of this step, it would be beneficial to discuss with them and create a list of things these individuals know, consolidating it across all your team members. As we discussed, at a given point in time, this persona is likely to be at one of the two extreme ends. Here are some of the common 'whats' we would like to know about:

- Different AI tools and technologies they have heard about.
- The capabilities of AI, according to them, in their domain and role.
- What they heard someone else is doing with AI.
- Are they 'for' or 'against' the push of AI from their leadership and their own reasoning?

Additionally, for the flavor of 'for' AI, some specific topics could come out, such as:

- Their recommendations or suggestions on where they want to use AI.
- The biggest possible transformations AI has to offer.
- The biggest proponents and wins of AI so far, according to them.

Similarly, for the flavor of 'against' AI, here could be some relevant questions:

- What are the biggest problems someone has seen with AI?
- What do they fear most about AI?
- What should the leadership and organization stay away from?

Learning the 'why' underneath

Just the 'what' might not give you the whole picture. It is important to learn the 'why' too. 'Why' is an excellent ingredient to be able to truly understand someone and being able to put oneself in their shoes. This, in the long run, helps us become a more empathetic leader, as well as helps with the right kind of dialogue and tailoring one's solutions and pitch accordingly.

While noting down the various 'whats' mentioned in the previous section, ask them the reason they think it is like that. The important thing here is to remain non-judgmental and objective when asking the question, as well as channeling your reaction and response to their answers.

Learning the 'why' is also a first step in differentiating their genuine conviction from their attempt to conform or overcome FOMO when it comes to popular opinion and wisdom.

Learning the 'how' as well

The picture is incomplete without the third important 'W' word: the 'how'. In this context, we should also try to learn a bit about how they know what they know and how their opinions and beliefs are being shaped.

The attempt here is to learn about the primary 'sources' of information the person aligns with and follows. This would typically be different for each person and is an important aspect of channeling their enthusiasm and direction. As covered before, a typical example of such a 'source' could be one or more of:

- Their slightly senior peers.
- A revered senior leader in the organization or in the industry.
- An influencer they follow.
- A specific social media or broadcasting channel.

Note: **This is for each of the people on your team during the conversation. All of the information captured for each person should be later triangulated and correlated to form takeaways and patterns leading to tailored solutions and direction.**

Managing their expectations

As a manager, it is imperative to have a dialogue with this set of team members about realistic and practical things to expect from AI and the changes it can really bring, both positive and negative. Hence, a good next step after gathering the above-mentioned data is to educate and streamline their expectations.

Channeling their curiosity

As a manager, having team members who are curious and eager to learn is a great privilege and a matter of great luck. The manager should try their best to ensure that these traits can stay alive for as long as possible in their careers before their opinions start to solidify into concrete ones, as they start to worry about alignment and conformance with the rest of the organization and with the long timers around.

For driving changes that are hard to get through, curiosity is one of the best tools to have, and hence, one should encourage, support, and reward this behavior as much as possible. Here are some of the ways to do this:

- Champion their participation in hackathons and greenfield projects.

- Pairing them for reverse mentoring with the other two personas we will study later in the book.

- Facilitating and conducting meet-ups and collaborations with other team members and a broader set of individuals with matching personas.

Leveraging the 'how' we learnt earlier

In the earlier part of this chapter, we learnt about the various reasons and channels that these team members are relying on as their source of information, as well as for building their opinions. The manager should try to leverage that information and those channels further.

They can do it in a few ways:

1. Firstly, learn what the most influential people and factors in the organization and society are.

2. Then, start to stay current with those, too.

3. Find ways to ensure that those are sharing accurate and objective information regarding AI.

4. Finally, utilizing those in their future plans for sharing their own directions and vision for their team for higher effectiveness.

Balancing the extreme ends

As in life, too much of anything is not really good. While we will have a systematic way of fundamentally controlling the wild sways, one should also nip extreme cases in the bud, balancing them back toward the middle.

Here are some tips on what to do when you see significantly 'for' AI opinions:

- Drive them to take it all the way. Find a way to get them to try AI in those scenarios, even in some small capacity. This will hopefully bring out the other side of the story, too, for them to learn from and form a more balanced view.

- Another thing you can do is to list some of the parameters and metrics of success for the scenario under question, and then help them map the impact of AI on that scenario. They will learn that the blessings of AI will not come without its side effects and 'cons'.

Similarly, when you see some extremely 'against' AI opinions, here is what to do:

- Just as in the previous point, help them recognize AI's revolutionary and positive impact on improving various success metrics.

- Encourage them to try some of the AI solutions in their own day-to-day work scenarios and help them see the benefits. AI typically does not have to bring just a small and incremental change; hence, this should help them get 'wowed' and learn the many benefits of AI, complementing the 'cons' they initially thought it had. Their negative perception about AI will likely appear more minor or relatively inconsequential, given all the positives they ended up experiencing in their own world.

Help control the sway

Authentic and practical learning will greatly help these team members form more stable and grounded opinions about AI. Additionally, in general, it will help them build their own personality and opinions by both challenging and incentivizing them to do so. Typically, this aligns well with building leadership skills and individuality. Feeling comfortable in 'conformance' may also indicate a lack of inclusion culture within the team. Hence, for a manager, this might also be a good opportunity to invest in building and fostering diversity and inclusion within themselves and their team.

Educating them on tools and use cases of AI

The next step in this journey with this persona would be to help fill in the blanks of the knowledge and opinions with more accurate and objective information.

Becoming the matchmaker

The easiest and most obvious way to do this would be to establish a connection between them and the more knowledgeable members and experts within the organization and the team. This is easier than it seems, and one of the ways to do it is to make it rewarding for both the parties to do this.

For the 'experts', some of the incentives could be the following:

- Giving them some goals and deliverables to drive, which will motivate them to tag-team with others to train and leverage them for these deliverables.

- A golden opportunity to influence and spread their expertise and beliefs.

- A long-awaited liberation from the constant pursuit of delivering business goals.

For the erstwhile wide-eyed ones, some of the ways this can be made attractive could be as follows:

- Incentivizing them to become more productive in their day-to-day by leveraging AI.

- Pride in being able to enable the seasoned 'experts' to deliver these critical goals.

- A golden opportunity to get time and resources for learning the cutting-edge set of things that add value to their experience and raise their market value.

- Bragging rights among their peers in similar organizations as they become the learned ones.

Driving them towards learning

In the previous chapter, we talked about the importance of learning for a manager as well as some suggestions on how to go about it. On similar lines, having done that for themselves, the manager can do the same for the team members of this persona too. This will likely be even more effective, given that these individuals come from a more receptive and curious mindset.

To recall, some of the ways we discussed were as follows:

- Meet-ups and seminars.
- Online courses and training.
- Sponsoring time and money for learning.
- Idea generation and hackathons: driving or participating.

Some additional ways for your team to think of are:

- Dedicated days of learning in a month.
- Encouraging a culture of prototyping and experimenting.
- Forums for cross-pollination via presenting and demonstrating their work or prototypes across silos.
- As a manager, walking the talk by doing some of these yourself, and then sharing the work or pulling in team members to take it forward.

Redirect them to more trustworthy channels

As a manager, you already have a good list and hints around the most popular and influential channels that this persona relates to. You can now do good homework by observing these popular channels and filtering out the real and trustworthy ones from those that are either someone's propaganda or run by fake influencers, who themselves are neither associated with nor experts in AI and its applications. The time and effort you, as the manager, will invest in doing this will yield multi-fold returns.

Some possible steps you, as the manager, can take in this direction are as follows:

1. Try to find the background and more information about the creators or owners by visiting their professional profile, network, and social media profiles.

2. See who they follow; it says a lot about their intentions and purpose.

3. Gather information about which content of others they have reposted, commented on or reacted. This can further bring up their interests and purpose.

4. Infer the tonality, choice of words, and sentiments they have used for their communication anywhere. This can also help filter out content from fluff or agenda, which is not constructive towards educating others and making things better.

Putting those diverse heads together

One other way to leverage and spread the existing knowledge in the system is to put diverse folks together. Not only can this be a useful tool for a manager in the context of AI, but it can also be used in other scenarios where you encounter islands of knowledge or beliefs within your team.

Some of the methods a manager can use are discussed in the subsections to follow.

Debate it out

A debate-style idea generation session where you can divide the team into discussing an upcoming AI tool or technology from a 'for' and 'against' points of view. Participating in this debate and simply by sitting and listening to counter opinions and information, they will be able to balance their opinions a lot more than they otherwise would have done.

To make it more effective and interesting, you can pick a few folks and encourage them to represent the other side of their current orientation, too. This will foster them to put themselves in the opposite shoes from their beliefs. Thus, they are likely to learn to appreciate and get educated on next level details they might have overlooked in favor of the importance of the channel they get their information from, such as the count of followers of the influencer they follow.

Write it down

It is common wisdom that when one writes down something, they remember or learn it more effectively and retain the information for a longer period. Foster a culture of writing down and running things by others. This encourages the individual to structure their thoughts and distil them in a consumable manner.

They would be required to come up with data and reasoning for their particular AI orientation. As a result, they will become more grounded and balanced and, sometimes, be able to identify the gaps in their knowledge. It will also help them supplement the information coming purely from the influencer or social platforms with facts and data.

As the manager, you can define the template for such documents to include sections for both pros and cons, as well as a space to conclude with how the final decision was arrived at after weighing them both objectively and scientifically.

Fieldwork

One of the most productive and fulfilling activities a team can undertake is to go into the 'field' and interact with reality. In this context, it could involve talking to customers or experts who are building or consuming similar products and services to those your team builds and sells. Asking the consumers or experts what they think AI can bring to these products and services, and what they would like to see transformed with AI, could be a great source of grounding knowledge as well as getting useful inputs for building your product and services roadmap in general!

On a related note, getting them to sit with some of the customers in the field to observe and learn how their products and services are being used will also help the individuals put their superpower of curiosity and learning to good use. They are sure to come back enriched and grounded, as well as full of real applications and ideas. As the manager, you can encourage them to share these insights with you and the team, helping to build various avenues for utilizing AI or identifying places where you previously planned to deploy AI but now find less useful or important based on the customer and data they have collected.

Conclusion

In this chapter, we dived deeper into the first of the three personas we have defined from an AI perspective. We learned nuances and characteristics of this persona and discussed the methods and dimensions of helping them move in the proper and objective direction from the AI side of things. And in the process, we also touched on building a more inclusive culture: a culture wherein the individuals in the team are not shy of being themselves to be successful and grow, and one where diverse opinions are not only supported, but rather, are encouraged.

In the next chapter, we will look at the second persona out of these three, and do a similar exercise in their respective context.

Join our Discord space

Join our Discord workspace for latest updates, offers, tech happenings around the world, new releases, and sessions with the authors:

https://discord.bpbonline.com

CHAPTER 4
Type B, the AI Enthusiasts

Introduction

In this chapter, we will try to learn more about the second of the three personas we have categorized the team members into, from an AI orientation perspective. For easy reference, the book will refer to them as 'Type B', that is, the AI enthusiasts, as they are very pro-AI.

As pointed out in the previous chapter, the book does not intend to stereotype or profile certain individuals. The objective is actually to be able to learn more about another segment of your team and try to put yourself in their shoes. This will be a key first step and a crucial one, to be able to get the best out of them and your team, as we will see in this and the later chapters of the book.

Structure

This chapter covers the following topics:

- Identifying and defining this persona
- Grounding their expectations

- Fixing the fitting problem to the solution syndrome
- Morphing them to be ambassadors of the AI revolution

Objectives

In this chapter, we will provide insight into how a specific type of team member thinks, what motivates them, and what doesn't. We will also outline a strategy to get them on board with the AI journey in an organic way and utilize their alignment to motivate and drive others.

Identifying and defining this persona

Just like we did in the previous chapter about the Type A persona, let us look deeper and identify a few signs of the Type B persona. Team members can be identified by some of the signs or behaviors listed as follows. As we will see, this persona is similar to the Type A persona in their believer phase. At the same time, they are different because their beliefs are more permanent and more grounded than the Type A persona in the believer mode. Some of the possible examples of who in your team might belong to this persona are as follows:

- Someone who has lot of industry experience and has a great acumen and curiosity for technology in general.
- Up-and-coming professionals who have grown-up with the AI way and are passionate about the same.

Person with opinions

One of the typical traits to spot could be that many of these folks are highly opinionated on most topics, especially those of a technical nature. You can typically see them chiming in directly or indirectly on any technical deep-dives, code reviews, or leadership presentations when roadmaps or directions are being shared. They typically bring in a completely different direction or information, especially technical or AI ones, many times uninitiated ones.

Their opinions and reactions typically emerge from the fact that they are well entrenched and well versed in the technical world, and in the AI dimension in this case. Additionally, as they are passionate about technology (in this case, AI), they will invariably react every time something is presented to them that either aligns with their existing knowledge or contradicts their thinking or information, and perhaps they have a better way to do it.

This makes it considerably easier to spot a Type B persona. Again, we do not attempt to profile or single out anyone, but the purpose is to be able to have the right kind of conversations with them later, as well as effectively utilize their skills and strengths for a win-win outcome. While it might look like a problem, being highly opinionated is actually really helpful in many circumstances because it signals clarity of thought. The managers can utilize this strength to devise a path forward in situations where there is a lot of ambiguity and no clear winning option is available. We will also talk about how the manager can utilize this in the context of AI in this and later chapters.

Expert on most things AI

Whether someone can be considered an 'expert' on something is subjective. No one can be deemed to know all about something. In the context of this conversation, being an expert indicates that someone is significantly more well versed on something (AI in this case) as compared to an average team member and thus, can be considered for taking an 'expert opinion' in place of finding out the most accurate and latest information about AI themselves.

Individuals belonging to this persona would have been working on or reading extensively about AI and its applications. Hence, they are well versed in the actual capabilities and use cases of AI and bring expert-like knowledge to the table. For this reason, when they talk about AI or are providing their inputs on its applications, they will come across as an expert as well as a reliable and authoritative source.

In most cases, their advice or choice would be something that you, as the manager, can take on face value at least from a technical perspective. Hence, you can rely on them to do some of the heavy lifting on your behalf and can directly work with the other team members on most things AI instead of you having to spend a significant amount of your time to orchestrate or channel things.

True believers in AI

In general, the book does not want to imply that someone in a complete black-and-white manner would be either completely 'for' or completely 'against' something no matter what. However, in reality, we as humans are generally polarized and choose one side over the other on most matters in most situations.

So, the meaning of 'true believer' here is that these folks have significantly positive opinions about AI and see it as something that is here to make things better. They would have either been working on the evolution of AI in their careers or the productivity, convenience, or sophistication it brings to our lives. They would have typically already been using or studying AI and its applications, and would be generally in touch with the latest happenings and advancements too.

Looking for problems to fit the AI solution

This might be a bit of stereotyping on the part of the book, making it possible and easy to spot this persona, but it is intentional, as some aspects of this can be observed in practice if you look.

We are all aware of the phrase 'fitting solution to the problem'. This phrase explains the act of ensuring that one keeps the problem they are solving in the center of their thinking and ensures that the solution they have chosen solves the problem completely and satisfactorily. Solving the problem is the key objective in this paradigm. This also implies finding and choosing the right solution and technology for that given problem. In other words, technology is a means to an end, not the end itself.

A reverse tendency we see in many technology enthusiasts is what we call the 'fitting problem to the solution'. Essentially, we try to find the problems to solve, with which the solution or technology we want to use can be fitted. In this paradigm, the centerpiece is the technology (the 'solution', that is), not the problem. The person is looking to apply the technology they like and put it to good use. It is like when we learn a new word in the language and try to use it in sentences as soon as possible and as much as possible: in the bargain, we are not speaking the way we should or normally do, but rather maximizing the usage of the word we just learned!

In this context, folks who are in love with AI would try to incorporate AI everywhere and try to find the problems they can use AI for, even if those problems are not the most important ones to solve for them, the customers, or the organization.

Grounding their expectations

As we discussed in the previous chapter, it is essential for managers to maintain an open mind and a learning mindset and to engage in dialogue with team members to dig deeper. Communication is always the key in both positive and challenging scenarios.

Moreover, this dynamic goes both ways. As a manager and an individual, you have your own beliefs and preferences, so an unbiased and objective dialogue can be a great opportunity to challenge your own knowledge and direction.

In this section, we will discuss some of the key topics and streams tailored towards this persona to have a dialogue with.

Having a dialogue about goals and metrics

Taking a cue from 'fitting problems to the solution' phenomenon, it is important to create awareness and have a dialogue about what truly matters and the purpose of the team's existence in the organization in the first place. Even for a team and company building technology, there are goals and metrics to define and measure success and impact. Therefore, these goals and metrics are generally a good framework for aligning prioritization and align on activities to spend time on.

It would be a good idea to talk to them, with more of a learning and curious mindset as a manager, to assess whether they are aware of the goals and success metrics for the team and organization in general. If they are, then it is a great place to be!

If they are not, it is good to educate them about it by sharing any memos, planning documents, or, in general, pointing to a previous leadership communication, and so on. As a manager, this is something you should also figure out a way to do organically and with the larger team so that everyone, not just this set of personas, is kept informed and in sync about the mission and measures for the team and the organization's work.

The purpose behind doing this is to establish the focal point for the rest of the narrative and go forward thinking about AI in the team. Having a shared understanding of the goals and success measures will help everyone self-govern in prioritization and potentially balance out a technology-first and impact-first approach in the right way.

Making it real and getting them to learn themselves

Let us now combine the two themes of technology-first, as well as goals and metrics.

It might be a valuable exercise to motivate and task these team members with exploring innovative solutions and return with proposals that enable the team to achieve their goals, including utilizing AI more effectively or in new ways. Essentially, start by giving them what they want and see if you find a win-win solution.

This approach can give dividends in many different ways:

- Utilizing the excellent expertise and knowledge of the AI enthusiasts to truly uncover better and productive solutions to your team's or product's biggest bottlenecks.

- Build trust and confidence in these team members, ensuring that their manager and the organization truly believe in them and are serious about embracing innovation and continuous improvement.

- Subconsciously, in everyone's mind, you, as the manager, are also paving the path for the future in terms of the culture within your team, where folks will be encouraged to come to you with new proposals and ideas. Thus, taking your team's stock up in the eyes of everyone.

- Last, but not least, you will become a manager people want to work for, as word-of-mouth about constructive and innovative managers and teams spreads very fast!

Raising awareness of the problems at hand

In addition to goals and metrics, which typically come from the business, customers, or leadership, top-down or outside-in, there are many challenges and problems that exist in each team but are not easily visible. Many of these are part of the 'implementation details' of delivering the goals.

These could also be things that are not directly connected with the business objectives but are affecting the team and team members in some way. These challenges or inefficiencies may be slowing the team down, compromising the quality of the work, or eroding the team's culture. The ultimate result of this might be that the team is not operating at its full potential.

Some of the examples are as follows:

- A large number of bugs are being found in production or by customers, thus randomizing and slowing down the team as they must stop their planned work of adding new features and instead spend time debugging and fixing these bugs.

- The time taken from writing code to getting it running in production is long and is slowing down the team's velocity. The leadership is not happy with this, as we are losing to our major competitor, as they are able to churn, say, 40% faster.

- Debugging a bug can take a very long time because the code is not intuitive and lacks clear comments.

- New hires in the team find it hard to get to full productivity for many months, owing to a lot of tribal knowledge and a lack of consumable information or documentation.

- A significant amount of time and effort is invested in providing status updates to various layers of leadership. Despite that, leaders do not feel they are up-to-date on the latest status of key things.

- The current programming language used for the product is now outdated, slowing the team down in adding new features and not supporting newer requirements easily. More and improved options exist in the world, but it will take us six months if we want to migrate to them. Moreover, the team cannot afford to put all resources into that by stopping or slowing down current work in any significant manner.

Fixing the syndrome

This topic deserves a dedicated section of its own and is clearly one of the major next steps and challenges to weed through. In the previous section, we attempted to take the first step of creating awareness and setting the ground for this step. Now, let us build on that to address what we are calling a 'syndrome,' as it is not necessarily specific to the topic of AI and may also have many other unwarranted side effects within a team.

Shiny object tendency and the problem therein

The problem-to-solution fitting topic can also be seen as a subset of the larger narrative: the shiny object scenario. Essentially, many individuals always want to be part of the most buzzworthy and talked about work streams. The kind of streams here include especially the ones containing the keywords the world is talking about or are considered 'cool'. And thus make their resumes attractive. Hence, the tag 'shiny object'.

Using AI solutions and fitting the problem to the solution can be a symptom of the shiny object tendency in general, too. This could be a talking point when discussing with the Type B persona. The manager should try to make them aware that this might be happening and that this might be a symptom of the larger shiny object problem. While having this conversation, do seek their view and hear their side of the story on this too in order to prevent confirmation bias on your part.

The book encourages you to discuss and align that this is something that the organization and team try to prevent. First and foremost, it does not help the purpose of our existence as a team. Moreover, it explains how and why it does not set the individuals, too, for success and growth.

Drawbacks of the solution first approach

Now that we have addressed the cultural element of this part, let us look at the more technical side and the problems with the solution first approach:

- For starters, this might not be the most important problem that exists in the team or product, but rather was chosen based on the solution that is readily available. Hence, even if the problem gets solved, the impact of doing all this work on the part of the individual will not be considered high, despite having put in all the hard work. This can also be thought of as a case of incorrect prioritization or priority inversion altogether.

- Secondly, if one has a solution (or technology at hand) and is looking for a problem to fit it, one is missing out on other better possible solutions and technologies that exist. Hence, their knowledge or experience will be incomplete.

- Thirdly, the problem one is trying to solve might not be getting solved in part or in full because one is not focusing on that to begin with. Hence, even after doing all the hard work and going through the solution, the problem might still exist, or any gaps will manifest in other ways.

- And last but not the least, let us say this was one of the top priority problems. In that case, someone else might need to put in effort in parallel to solve the problem because the above solution is not the best for it. Hence, as a team, we are spending double the effort to solve, which not only wastes our effort but also slows us down overall in terms of output.

The book recommends using one or more of these talking points to discuss and nudge the Type B into a more balanced direction.

Channeling this into something constructive

While it may sound like techno-enthusiasm is all bad, let us try to balance it out and explore the positive side.

One of the important aspects of prioritizing technology and AI is that it enables one to explore all possibilities and uncharted spaces. Placing it within the constraints of a problem can sometimes restrict creativity and innovation, especially when it comes to a once-in-a-generation revolution like AI.

As a manager, you can make a judgment call about possibly approaching this from a different angle, rather than just from the perspective of AI being a solver for the problems you see on the horizon. So instead, or in addition to grounding the potential too soon, a manager can go in the opposite direction. The recommendation here is to nudge the Type B teammate in a different direction: that of exploration and 'revolution'. However, you should choose this option if the person in question has a really good past track record, credibility, and credentials.

The suggestion is to have a dialogue with them and reiterate faith in their expertise, enthusiasm and eagerness to put AI to good use. Explain to them that this is a great opportunity for them and for the team to reshape the future using AI in a major way as opposed to smaller wins and 'incremental' successes.

It is important to confirm if they are up for it as well as ensure them that you have their back in case things do not go well or no major breakthrough comes out. It will at least ensure that they are able to exercise their fullest potential, curiosity and leave nothing unexplored. By doing this, the team member is very likely to feel heard, supported, as well as energized to take this forward. Additionally, going forward, this can help form a stronger bond between the two of you!

One important aspect is to ensure that the outcome remains measurable in some way and that there is a sense of accountability on the individual, even though we are talking about letting them loose, so to speak.

Morphing to be ambassadors of the AI revolution

To work on action item planning, as covered later in the book, there are a few prerequisites we need to meet beforehand. We will need the support and active involvement of all team members in the AI transformation journey. Just as we did for Type A individuals towards the end of the previous chapter, let us examine the role Type B will play in this and how we can guide them towards it.

Building on the strengths and orientation of Type B team members, they are well-suited to be ambassadors and torchbearers for the AI revolution within the team and the product. Let us have a look at some of the ways to nudge them to play that role.

Referencing the competitive landscape

It will be a good idea to get them to pull their neck out of their world and look around to know what others are doing. The 'others' here could be their other team members, other members in the larger organization, the competitors, or the world at large.

You can nudge or task them with studying the competitive landscape, even purely from a technology-first and AI-first lens, and compare notes. Additionally, you can give them a goal to follow-up with a comparative study. This could include identifying the pros and cons and sharing their findings and recommendations with you, the team, or leadership, either as a presentation, a set of demos, or notes and documents.

One of the primary benefits of this approach for you, as a manager, and the team will be to gain a more comprehensive understanding and recommendations for AI technologies and use cases, as well as get an equal footing or a head start on the competition from the get-go.

The other benefit for Type B will be that they will have the opportunity to broaden their mind, learning more than just what they already think or know, and also ground and channel their knowledge and recommendations by utilizing industry-wide knowledge. This is likely to make them aware of possible blind spots in their knowledge or approach, as well as ground them as both professionals and humans.

From the sidelines to the frontline

Not to stereotype, but chances are that these folks prefer to play more of a role of observing and reporting as opposed to jumping in and being one with the real stuff on the ground. The reason for this conclusion is that these folks are typically trying to do their own stuff and are driven and energized by technology and are one with it. Due to their positive energy towards AI in this case, they are ideal for driving everyone along with it. Think of this as the quietly sitting 'potential energy' that we need to turn into 'kinetic energy'.

Any change or transformation requires a lot of positive energy to be infused into the team. That energy can come quickly from these individuals, who are enthusiastic about AI and eager to explore any opportunity to get started with all things AI. As a manager, you can show them the direction to make a significant impact, and also join hands with them in finding challenges and problems. This cannot be done from sitting on the sidelines. You can use some of these points to motivate and nudge them to jump right in and step out of the shadows to the center stage in driving various conversations and projects involving AI transformation for the team. Landing the point about these directly connected with their own performance and impact is one of the most obvious ways to do this.

One point worth mentioning is about the individual personalities and preferences. Not every person of this persona will enjoy or possess the necessary qualities to thrive in the limelight, nor will they have the strongest people and communication skills. As a manager, you can evaluate on a person-by-person basis and provide confidence, coaching, or direct help on this aspect while the focus is on their technical skills and positivity above anything else.

Popular and pleasant voice

In continuation of the previous point, a true AI transformation down the line requires what is known as a **snowball effect**. In a field of snow, if you roll a very small ball of snow downhill, it keeps gathering more and more snow as it rolls and becomes larger and larger. It is a good strategy to drive any kind of major transformation in a team or project and AI transformation would be a fitting example here too.

In this context, it means starting with those who are already in favor and doing so, then picking the next layer and the next layer, and so on, to add to this momentum. Generally, the team members at large gravitate towards and connect well with folks who are on the side of technology and domain and not necessarily who speak the management-talk of business goals, metrics, process, constraints and so on.

Hence, it is highly likely that, even as an undercurrent, Type Bs are forming positive connections with other team members because they typically speak first about technology and AI. The other folks will find it hard to be the torchbearer themselves, but relatively easy to latch on to others who are taking the front seat, such as Type Bs in this case.

This approach can slowly and truly turn into an AI snowball wherein the initial small ball rolled out was Type Bs. The first set of folks to form the next layer of this snowball could be those who secretly want to go the AI route but are not the ones to take the first step. These Type Bs, bringing pleasant and popular voices, can very easily get these folks latched to the snowball.

This can go on in a rinse and repeat manner, where at each step, the next person who sees others joining the bandwagon can help them shed the inertia and attach to this AI snowball. There will be those who are not easily pulled like this, and we will need more deliberate efforts and thoughtful planning, as we will see in later chapters.

Conclusion

In this chapter, we explored the team members whom we termed the AI enthusiasts or Type B persona from a balanced point of view. We attempted to understand their perspectives, strengths, shortcomings, or blind spots from an AI perspective. We looked at some of these from a broader perspective to understand them and the scenario more holistically and to formulate our thoughts more fundamentally.

We explored several ways to raise awareness among them about the potential downsides of their beliefs and how to address these issues. We also discussed how we can prepare them to leverage and channel these strengths to shape the AI transformation for the team. Let us make a note of these ingredients, which will play a major role in the later part of the book, when we combine all of those to pave the path forward for the team's AI transformation.

In the next chapter, we will explore the third of the three personas to learn more about them and discuss the ways to make them part of the AI journey.

Join our Discord space

Join our Discord workspace for latest updates, offers, tech happenings around the world, new releases, and sessions with the authors:

https://discord.bpbonline.com

CHAPTER 5

Type C, the nAI-sayers

Introduction

In this chapter, we will try to learn more about the third and last of the three personas into which we have categorized the team members from the **artificial intelligence** (**AI**) orientation perspective. For easy reference, the book will refer to them as Type C, the nAI-sayers (pronounced as 'naysayers'), as they are against or not so supportive of AI.

As a reminder, the book does not intend to stereotype or profile certain individuals. The objective is actually to learn more about another segment of your team and try to put yourself in their shoes. This will be a key first step and a crucial one, to be able to get the best out of them and your team, as we will see in this and the later chapters of the book.

Structure

This chapter covers the following topics:

- Identifying and defining this persona

- Getting to the bottom of their skepticism
- Enriching with information to bridge the gap
- Connecting them with the other two personas

Objectives

In this chapter, we will try to build a fair idea about getting insight into how the third kind of persona in your team thinks, what works for them, and what does not. We will also strive to develop a strategy for guiding them through the AI journey in the most effective and organic manner. There will be a special focus on how to address their potential unfavorable stance on AI. We will then look at how to create a balanced dialogue and scenario for the maximum impact and a win-win situation for them and the team.

Identifying and defining this persona

Just like we did in the previous two chapters about the Type A and B personas, let us look deeper and identify a few signs of the Type C persona. Team members belonging to this persona can be identified by some of the signs or behaviors listed as follows.

As we will see, this persona is similar to the Type A persona in their non-believer phase. At the same time, they differ because their beliefs are more enduring than those of the Type A persona in the non-believer mode. However, we must note that, unlike Type B, where we believed that the persona was formed by grounded knowledge of AI and its applications, here, it is not necessarily a factor in forming their opinions.

Status quo first

One of the possible and obvious signs indicating strong pushback against AI might be that these folks are generally much more comfortable with the status quo on most things and averse to change in general. We should acknowledge that we, as humans, by and large crave 'the familiar' and a 'change' is never what we want, if given a choice. However, an extreme case of this is when someone would like to keep things as they are, even if presented with an option for making things better. Their challenge of change might also emanate from the fear of the unknown, which comes with any change, especially a major one like AI.

Type Cs might generally try their best to maintain the status quo on most things and may want to find ways to resist or oppose change, either openly or in a more passive manner. It is not that they might never adopt change, but rather that they generally require a lot of convincing, follow-ups, and a clear carrot or stick approach to accept change. They might end up accepting change not because they think it is a good change, but because it is required for their existence, job security, or because the policy mandates it. In many ways, this can also be qualified as a 'fixed mindset' (as opposed to a 'growth mindset').

Why fix it if it is not broken

A person of the Type C persona, more often than not, might ask something like this when they are presented with constructive feedback in general, or the team is trying to embrace something new. They would argue that everything is working as expected, so why try to fix anything? What if the change makes it worse instead of the intended improvement? This is similar to the status quo point and is one of the easier ways to spot the Type Cs 'in action'.

In reality, we all make this tradeoff of looking at the best-case upside and worst-case downside of most new things; however, different personas lean differently based on the central sentiment. In the case of Type Cs, inertia or a lack of enthusiasm for new ways may lead them to resist improvements, especially if something has been running a certain way for a long time and is in a steady state, working fine.

Non-believer in AI or technology

Many of us are used to relying on the manual way of doing something, even if technology has evolved and can help out with a portion or complete part of the task. This can spring from a general fear of the 'worst-case scenario' of technology failing or the feeling of losing control if we are not able to see the details of how the task is being done with our own eyes. Technology of any kind, in general, is indeed prone to failure and can often result in a catastrophe as well. In the case of AI, the traditional perception at large, though, is that AI always goes rogue in the end and turns against humanity. One factor that might have potentially contributed to this perception is the stereotypical portrayal of AI in numerous prominent sci-fi movies, such as the *Terminator* or *Avengers* franchise, as emotionless killing machines.

This fear is not completely unfounded because we do have many real examples of AI, such as **generative AI (GenAI)**, getting out of control. We have seen chatbots gradually starting to use harmful or offensive language for long conversations when involving controversial topics. Many recent versions of chatbots were also seen hallucinating and blurting out wrong and misleading information when the training data did not have sufficient information to provide the correct answer. In other examples, while AI did not malfunction on its own, users could drive it into jailbreak and force it to use abusive, irresponsible, or harmful tone or language. Another promising use case of AI is self-driving cars, and we keep getting reports of them running into major accidents every now and then. The fact that AI companies continually have to invest in building safety systems to prevent these errors is also an indication that this is not just a perception.

The Type Cs typically might over-index on the worst-case scenarios of technology, including AI, even if the odds are very small of that happening. Therefore, they might be ignoring the benefits and advancements it brings in the majority of cases or the best-case scenarios. This might be a possible strong factor in them not being supporters of using AI.

Getting to the bottom of their skepticism

Staying true to the growth mindset, the book recommends starting by learning more and keeping an open mind, rather than being judgmental or jumping to conclusions. To think of it in another way, as the manager, we should take our own advice of keeping a growth mindset even when dealing with the fixed mindset demonstrated by the Type C teammates!

We should try to learn and isolate the sources and reasons for the Type C team members being a nAI-sayer. Let us examine some steps and key dimensions to approach this.

Having a dialogue to learn more

As always, 'tell me more' is a good place to start. Taking a cue from their past record and how they generally operate, the manager can formulate their questions accordingly. Generally, try to first understand what they think about AI and assess whether they are grounded or basing their views on the vox populi and traditional perceptions of negativity. Next, it is also beneficial to examine whether their opinions are specific to AI or if they are generally resistant to change and new ways of doing things. This is best accomplished through a series of one-on-one conversations, ideally conducted in close succession. At a higher-level, we are trying to determine whether they are averse to the problems being solved or specifically to the solutions involving AI.

Connecting and empathizing

Finding common ground to 'connect' and genuinely empathize with them is a great starting point and gesture on the part of the manager. Do have a close conversation and genuinely be able to say that you understand where they are coming from. This would be a great first step after learning the roots of their beliefs.

As a manager, in most cases, if your teammate's opinions are very different from your own beliefs, it might be a good strategy to take a step back and try to put yourself in their shoes. This might include transporting yourself to their perspective, finding supporting arguments and reasons for their views, and, in a way, convincing yourself that their thoughts might also be correct. Essentially, a manager should wholeheartedly trust the team member to have good reasons for forming their opinions and beliefs and put themselves in their world to experience what they are experiencing.

Discussing efficiency, productivity and a better way

We should determine the talking points here, depending on whether the Type Cs are averse to the problems we are trying to solve, or whether AI is the solution (refer to the earlier paragraphs).

Case 1: In case problems are the centerpiece

Let us take the case where the teammate is not aligned even with the problems we are trying to solve. In that case, as the manager, you should direct them to things that matter and are essential for impact and success, essentially the whats and whys.

Educate them and create awareness regarding the various metrics, including those around efficiency and productivity, that we need to improve on. Explain why those are important and seek their alignment on the fact that they, too, agree that these problems are crucial and make sense to solve for the team and product. If needed, refer to leadership memos, customer data, product requirements, and other relevant materials to effectively convey the point.

Case 2: In case of AI being the solution is the centerpiece

If the teammate is aligned that the problems we are trying to solve need to be solved now, but they do not think AI is the right way to go, then the manager should take an additional or different approach.

In this case, stepping back and asking for their inputs or recommendations on the best solutions to solve this, without trying to oversell AI, would be a good way to break the deadlock. It might seem to slow down the whole process; however, this is expected to result into a more permanent and deep alignment going forward and a more effective and pleasant way of doing things in the long-term.

If, as a result of this conversation, both of you came up with a better solution to the given problem, then it is a great outcome even though the result does not involve applying AI to it. The reason is that we should try to not fit the problem to the solution but the other way around. Chances are that in most cases, it will be hard to find a solution that is much more effective, efficient, attractive, and future-proof than what the AI version of the solution offers.

Making them aware of the world's reality

Let us also come from another angle, outside-in, if you may. We live in the real-world, and change is the only constant. The real-world is moving fast, and everyone is trying to be one step ahead of the others in the adoption of AI and AI-fying everything. Survival of the fittest continues to be the way nature works, and AI wave is no different.

Let us examine two of the broader points we recommend discussing with the Type C persona. Try to make them aware of these real aspects and nudge them to introspect and come to their own version of acceptance of the world's reality. It might not happen in a single conversation and might need a series of dialogues. Reaching this stage will be a valuable milestone for both managers and teams, as it ensures that the majority of team members, especially Type Cs, share a clear understanding of the situation and a unified commitment to the common mission.

Ground under us is moving

Even if we try to stick to tried and tested traditional tools, technologies and methods, the world is moving forward and resulting in those either not being available anymore or being evolved into their AI-fied versions. Even in our day-to-day lives, we will automatically be getting moved to AI-based everyday things, whether we try or not and whether we like it or not. Just like time moves on its own and we do not have a choice to remain in the current time. We automatically move to the new hour, day and year. Similarly, any technical advancement moves the world forward, irrespective of any individual trying their best not to move forward, since the 'past' cannot exist! It is like someone saying they do not want to circle around the sun, because that is not possible, considering the earth on which they stand is revolving around the sun, and as a result, they are inherently also doing the same.

Skillset landscape is evolving rapidly

From a skillset and job definition perspective, AI has brought about an extremely rapid movement, and more seems to be on the horizon. Hence, those professionals, in any field of work, who are immune to the advancements in AI in their respective fields are very likely to either get stuck in their careers or worse, not being employable anymore.

Enriching with information to bridge the gap

So far in this chapter, the objective was to get to a common ground with the Type Cs and get to mutual 'generic' alignment, also known as **in-principle alignment**. This is very important as this lays the foundation of creating a conducive environment for further conversation and planning. Now, we will build on that and delve into specifics to further develop this.

As the first step, we will attempt to build a knowledge base about AI by making all possible information about AI available to them and facilitating their learning. We will go about it in a few different dimensions, as explained further.

Tools and technologies

The first dimension is the various tools and technologies that AI is bringing. This will be specific to the area of work the team or the individual is in. As a manager leading this team, it will be a good idea to compile a list of the various tools and technologies that you would like every team member to learn, and the same can be made available to Type Cs too. Depending upon their degree of acceptance as well as knowledge gap, you can provide not just a list but also a more detailed set of resources like videos, documents, tutorials, and so on.

One excellent help to the team could be if you could come up with a 'guided tour' around this, so that folks can easily know the order in which they should learn these tools and the pace they should try to go with. Organizing this into weekly, fortnightly, and monthly milestones will be a very intuitive and effective way to do this. This will also help individuals be self-driven in their learning and can share frequent updates with you on their progress, as opposed to you having to drive and follow-up from your end.

Competitive landscape

Learning from competition is generally a great strategy and we can utilize the same for building AI literacy too! You can utilize the competitive study that your Type B might have done in the previous chapter and have the Type Cs spend time learning and understanding those.

You can even go a step further, as per feasibility. Encourage them to discover a similar list of tools and technologies your most significant competitor has for their source of learning and see how it compares to your list. You can even encourage them to challenge the learning plan you have built by bringing in a better one if they can! This will not only help them feel empowered, supported and treated as equals by their manager but also will help enrich and enhance the learning curriculum you have built.

Memos and roadmaps

Let us look at some of the possible resources that are available to you as the manager that you can leverage as a source of information and utilize directly or indirectly to educate your team.

Learning and internalizing the organization's vision

In almost every company and organization, leaders spend a significant amount of effort and time compiling and sharing their vision, goals, and mission statements with their team. Managers can benefit immensely from utilizing them. The recommendation is to read, understand, internalize, and try to link them to what your team is working on currently or has been tasked with in the future. These will likely include what the company and the organization is looking to achieve and which metrics or needles need to move from a business perspective. It is also likely to include a mission of adopting more AI, including the strategy of the organization to introduce AI in specific areas or tasks.

Asking questions and closing gaps in your understanding and knowledge in terms of what the leaders mean, how they recommend the organization to go about it, and also how it connects to what each of the parts of the unit are accountable for is a great goal to aim for.

Distilling the larger vision to team-specific level

After learning and internalizing these top-down directions and visions, you can attempt to create a translation or 'mapping' set of simplified documentation for your team, including adding things that are specific about your world but would not be covered in the broader memo. You can then use some of that in your team meetings and townhalls to explain and clarify, including a forum for your teammates to ask questions and get clarity. All in all, this will help the Type C to learn the 'what' and the 'why'.

Using roadmaps to pave the road forward

Coupled with memos are roadmaps and planning documents. Those can be a great source of information and learning about the 'how' and milestones the larger ship is trying to achieve. Similar to vision statements, you can also utilize these to learn the specifics of 'how' the larger organization plans to achieve its goals. You can create zoomed-in views of these that are specific to you and your team. You can then use these to educate your Type Cs on the 'hows' of using these.

Handling the possible lack of structured vision

It is possible that your organization does not have the practice of writing and building such formal alignment centrally. That is a blessing in disguise for you as a manager, as it presents an excellent opportunity to step up and compile one for your team. You can also seek support from the next higher-level of your organization's leadership to determine if they can address the issue at their level. This may involve defining important success metrics, as well as exploring how they envision AI playing a role and how they would like to adopt AI for their organization.

Training and workshops

It is a known adage that there are various modes of learning that complement each other in order to complete the circle of learning. Some of the modes of learning are listening, watching, reading, writing, or doing. The last one especially can help absorb and retain the knowledge for much longer and, can help open the person's mind to more possible ways and applications of the thing they are trying to learn.

As discussed in earlier chapters, even in this short period, there has been a flood of training and tutorials in the field of AI. A lot of trainers and organizations have done the hard work of creating easy-to-consume and digestible curated content and training, including hands-on exercises. You can facilitate such training for your team, especially for Type Cs.

In addition to the generic AI learning, you can also collaborate with other managers and the larger organization to conduct learning workshops, which can be both generic about AI as well as specific to the products, domain and technology that you and your sister teams are dealing with and can be much more productive and relevant for your team. This can be much more interesting and important for your team members to supplement and build on top of the generic AI learning.

Connecting them with the other two personas

Continuing the forward progress, following the 'in-principle' alignment, we grounded our approach in business goals and educated the Type Cs about AI and various tools. We can now utilize the next tool in our arsenal: the power of bringing many heads together. The other pre-steps we have done so far will form an essential base to ensure a fruitful and productive outcome of this step.

Before you simply put different personas in the same room and ask them to exchange knowledge and ideas, there are a few key things to consider. In addition to that, it will be good to take a partitioned and step-by-step approach. Let us discuss how to go about doing this.

Type As

You can start by connecting a Type C with a Type A. We recommend ensuring this is done only after achieving the previously mentioned alignment and at least a large part of information dissemination has been completed. We do this to ensure that the conversations are much more grounded in real information and beliefs as opposed to perception and hearsay.

Purpose and goals

The purpose of connecting these two personas is to help use the momentum, alignment and knowledge acquired by the Type Cs to impart the same onto Type As. Thus, benefiting from the snowball effect in relaying things that you, as the manager, work hard on building with Type Cs in the earlier part of this chapter. In addition, this also gives Type Cs the opportunity to test their newly acquired knowledge and logic with someone who is highly impressionable and essentially a clean slate. It is like when we solidify our learning of something by trying to practice things like 'how would you explain this to a 5 year-old'.

You can possibly pick the teammates to pair not just based on the persona but also utilizing any past synergy between the two as well as those who might be collaborating already by working on the same area or project. This will avoid any need for initial handshakes and ice-breaking, and instead, they can get straight to the conversation.

Few possible narratives

You can seed this conversation between the two by one or more of the following narratives. Let us say the Type A teammate in this conversation is called *Angela* and the Type C is called *Charlize*. The book chooses these names to make it easy to connect the person with the name, given that they share the first letter of their name with the persona type we are associating them with:

- *Hey Charlize, here is Angela! I learnt that Angela is curious about AI and has many questions. You as someone who has recently gone through the trainings and workshops, I thought would be the best person to spend some time with her to answer her questions. While you are at it, maybe you two can exchange ideas and possible ways we can benefit more from AI in our team or lives.*

- *Hey Angela, meet Charlize! She has some great in-depth knowledge and also shares the cautious stance you have about AI. Why do not you two gang-up and see what you both come back with? I am curious to know what you recommend to us in terms of where to use*

AI: and should we even go the AI way.

- *Angela and Charlize! Here are two of the amazing and energetic AI enthusiasts who I am lucky to have in my team! And what I love about this is that it truly represents excellence in having diverse opinions in one place, allowing us to stay balanced and thrive as an organization. On one hand, we have Angela, who is a smart and enthusiastic fresh grad and is someone who is social media savvy and can tell you all about who is saying what about AI! On the other hand, we have a much more well-read and self-opiniated Charlize who can help you weed the truth! Would you two like to go on a detective assignment of sorts to uncover the truth from the hype? And why do not you two bring me up to speed in 3 weeks as to what you find! Does that sound good?*

Type Bs

The next assignment you can take is to get Type C to meet-up with a Type B person.

Purpose and goals

The desired outcome here is to conduct a thorough cost-benefit and pros and cons analysis of AI in your short and long-term plans and develop a direction forward. This outcome can also help you do a reality check regarding whether you are biased. In addition, the plan, developed through the collaboration of strong team members, has a lot more substance and a higher chance of success, making it easier for the rest of the team to adapt.

The first thing that should come to your mind is that opposites attract. But is that really true in the case of two polar opposite team members and in this particular scenario of AI orientation? One thing is for sure: you are assured of sparks of some sort flying due to this interaction. However, since we have done some groundwork of educating and opening up the Type Cs as well as balancing the Type Bs tech-first approach, we should have a much more productive and positive outcome.

Similar to the interaction between Type A and Type C we saw in the previous pages, this interaction also needs a starting point, an agenda, and goals. Let us attempt to come up with these. For Type B, it is a good challenge to put their positive beliefs to the test by trying to interact with someone who is a skeptic and also has good knowledge about the subject, AI. For the Type C, it might be fascinating and interesting to interact with someone who thinks really positively about something they are not so positive about, such as AI.

Again, like the Type A and Type C interaction scenario, try to see if you can pick the two individuals who might have some level of familiarity, mutual respect, and connection. This will make it easier to get on the main agenda sooner, and also, the interactions and outcomes are likely to be more objective and productive.

Few possible narratives

Here are some possible sets of kick-offs you can do to put these interactions into motion. Let us suppose that the Type B is called *Bobbi*. For continuity and ease, let us stick to *Charlize* being our Type C in question:

- *Hey Charlize, I trust you already know Bobbi! Bobbi is our resident expert on AI and has been suggesting many exciting AI tools to us, as well as sharing numerous ideas on how we can make our team highly productive and savvy by leveraging AI. I thought it might be fantastic if you two can spend some time to analyze those in depth and come back to me with a consolidated set of recommendations and directions. I would love for you to do some sort of pros and cons analysis of various options and propose the winners of this analysis from your combined points of view.*

- *Hey Bobbi, this is Charlize. Charlize had really good constructive feedback about our grand AI plans I shared with you and the team couple of weeks ago. That gave me a window of opportunity of grounding this whole thing better. I want to step back and ensure that we as a team choose the right direction not because the manager wants it but because that stands the test of your analysis. It will be great if both of you can scrutinize the plans we reviewed recently and get back with a fair cost-benefit analysis and help us plan and prioritize our investments accordingly.*

- *Bobbi and Charlize. Here are two of the most excellent AI expert teammates I have had the privilege to have on my team! I would love for both of you to help us shape our AI narrative towards our team as well as towards the leadership. The leadership has been hearing all this mad buzz about AI around the world and is eager for us to be AI-enabled and not miss out on this golden opportunity. However, I need someone who can help us with bottoms-up thinking and expert analysis especially grounded in our kind of scenarios, use cases and domain. I would love for the two of you to brainstorm and get back to me with your recommendations. You can use the leadership memo as the platform for providing your inputs or if you want to completely start from scratch, that will be perfectly fine as well. But please try to make sure that you do not take too long. How does 2 weeks from now sound?*

Co-hacking and seminars

As the title suggests, the next obvious step could be to devise a creative and fun approach to the AI journey. You can put the *Angelas*, *Bobbies*, and *Charlizes* together in the team and encourage them to apply some of the ideas and theories they developed in the previous step. They can test the waters by building some quick and dirty prototypes, essentially 'hacking it out', if you will. You can choose to pair them up or put all three together, too, depending upon your best judgment.

In addition to co-hacking, you can also find opportunities for them to jointly conduct or participate in seminars and meet-ups relating to AI and new AI-enabled solutions and tools. As with hacking, it is best to pair the two of them or have the three of different kinds go at it together.

Conclusion

In this chapter, we dived deeper into possibly one of the hardest ones to crack, the Type Cs, the nAI-sayers. We discussed a few practical and collaborative approaches and ideas on how to go about getting through to them and building the bridge to build further plans on top of. We explored a few ideas that you, as a manager, can take on, and many others where you can use the power of teamwork by pairing them with the other two personas and using their help to create win-win proposals.

This concludes the trilogy of chapters covering the overall canvas of various possible demographic of your team members from an AI orientation perspective. This sets the foundation for thinking about the plan as the manager in your team's AI journey.

In the next section of the book, we will go about the AI transformation journey in a systematic manner. The next chapter will take up the first step of this transformation, namely the planning aspect. We will build on top of the learnings of both the AI-landscape and the in-depth understanding of our team members in order to embark on this conquest.

Join our Discord space

Join our Discord workspace for latest updates, offers, tech happenings around the world, new releases, and sessions with the authors:

https://discord.bpbonline.com

CHAPTER 6
Plan the Transformation

Introduction

So far in this book, we have put in efforts to learn more about the AI state of the world as well as about our team members. We will spend the next three chapters utilizing this knowledge to put things into motion. Each of the three chapters represents the three phases of the journey, respectively: the preparation, the execution, and moving to a self-sustained loop after this one-time progression.

This chapter aims to help with the preparation in terms of setting up an execution plan and related pieces. We will bring together the various artifacts and knowledge we have gathered in previous chapters and utilize them to come up with a tailored plan for your team and other things specific to your scenario.

Structure

This chapter covers the following topics:

- Taking a stock of things compiled so far

- Preparing narratives for leadership and team
- Establishing success criteria and metrics
- Deciding changes for 30-60-90-days

Objectives

In this chapter, we will move forward with realigning and setting your team up in the best way for the AI era. We already had some wheels in motion, and we will continue to build on top of those and fit then in a much more comprehensive way. As before, the book continues to take an objective and unbiased approach to everything, including AI. Owing to this, we will try to come up with a tailored approach that considers specifics for you and the team instead of assuming that the goal is to implement AI everywhere.

Taking a stock of things compiled so far

Before we begin preparing the plan, let us summarize the various ingredients we have gathered so far. There are three categories of things we have learned so far, and they are as follows:

- **The background:**
  - o AI world view.
  - o Framework for finding various ways AI can be used in a specific domain and team.

- **The 'who':**
  - o Identification of different possible personas in your team, categorized into three groups.
  - o Various tailored methods to engage different personas and take them along in the AI journey.
  - o Getting different personas to collaborate and learn from each other.

- **The artifacts and supporting material:**
  - o A possible list of metrics and measurable goals for your team from an AI perspective.

- o   A comprehensive list of trainings and tutorials on AI, tailored for your team.

- o   A few bottoms-up proposals, ideas, and prototypes of key problems and AI-based solutions for your team, many of them coming from your team members.

- o   A few key company-level memos and other documents that depict broader AI goals.

Preparing narratives for leadership and team

This might sound obvious, but as part of an organization, we work with other humans. Any plan or change needs us to create clarity and get them along in order to implement and succeed. One intuitive way to do that is to use storytelling for the different segments of the organization: the leadership above you and your team. We will typically need a separate narrative for each of these segments.

As is the case when driving any consensus, it is crucial to think about 'what is in it for them'. Hence, when we try to come up with our respective narratives for each participant, we should have this as the key guiding factor.

Key terms

Let us now go through a few terms that we will use to build our narrative. These terms were used in the book earlier in a subtle manner but now would be crucial points to structure your narrative. So, let us relearn them:

- **The 'what'**: This describes what exactly we are trying to achieve and how we will measure success or failure once we are done with the respective task. It is typically represented by numbers, metrics, and other measurable indices such as the number of monthly customers, revenue targets, cost per request served, and so on.

- **The 'why'**: This refers to the purpose and reason for doing something. It typically does not include numerical points but rather things like purpose, mission statement, objectives, and motivating factors for picking up a task or direction.

- **The 'how'**: This refers to the mechanics and implementation details of how the given goal or outcome will be achieved. This aspect gets into the details of various tools, technologies, designs, plans, processes, estimations, resource requirements, and other nuts and bolts.

- **The 'so-what'**: This is similar to the 'why', but the angle we are approaching is a bit more self-critical. Essentially, this refers to why something really matters. The point that subtly differentiates this from the 'why' is that 'why' can be a choice without any reasoning, but 'so-what' tries to view things from a grounded perspective and asks the hard question of what we will achieve if we do this. Another differentiator is that 'why' is generally an opening note of the march, whereas 'so-what' is a question you might ask after doing something.

- **'Outside-in' or 'top-down'**: We use this term typically to refer to goals or metrics coming from outside of the team. For instance, 'outside-in goals' will refer to the goals that the leadership or customers expect your team and product, respectively, to deliver. Another way to interpret this is that we are looking at our team as an opaque box and without getting into 'how' something is to be done, 'what' is this box supposed to deliver, or what the success measure for your team is.

- **'Inside-out' or 'bottoms-up'**: This term is typically used when we are referring to the goals or metrics coming from within the team. For example, the phrase 'inside-out goals' will refer to things that matter to the team but might not be about the business metrics. These goals typically do not conflict with the business goals and in fact are a result of defining the 'how' the team achieves those. These can vary from team to team depending upon the specific ownership, circumstances, team size and makeup of the team.

  A good example can be the goal of limiting meeting duration for the team to a total of 8 hours per week. A different team might restrict it to 12 hours because the nature of their work requires more meetings than the first team. In either case, as you can see, how many hours a team spends in a meeting per week would not be a business metric but more of how the team decides to operate to achieve their actual business goals and associated metrics.

Deciding the tone and crux of your story

The first thing to consider is the tone and focal point of your AI transformation story. As we will see next, there are several possible options. In practice, there might be a 'main plot' and one or more 'sub-plots' of the narrative, which will comprise one or more of the following possibilities.

Centered around business objectives

This is the case where your proposal is about business objectives being the paramount consideration, and how you suggest using AI to be the differentiator there. The book suggests using this tone and having your story revolve around this narrative in case one or more of the following scenarios are applicable:

- Your company and leadership obsess mostly about business objectives (the 'what' that is) and not significantly about the 'how'. The domain you are in might demand that you keep business objectives at the center.

- The business is in a steady state and not fighting for survival, but there is an opportunity to leapfrog and grow the business in a big way by doing more things or in a better way by using AI.

- Your product's use case is conducive and beneficial for customers in an AI-fied way. In other words, there are many functionalities, experiential or performance improvements that can be done by using AI in your product or solution.

- You see that the business objectives are ambitious, and it is harder to meet them without bringing in major change, such as AI.

- The product or solution you built has been in the market for ages and has a loyal customer base, but you see that the proportion of new signups or new-age customers is not increasing.

In this case, you would need to ensure that your narrative weaves around business goals and captures how it will help to advance business goals further. You will tell the story of why the leadership and the organization should invest in bringing in AI and changing things that are working fine. In essence, your narrative will be centered around the 'what' and 'so-what' and less about the 'how'.

Centered around productivity, efficiency and a better way

This is the case when things are happening in a satisfactory manner, but you see an opportunity to do them in a better way (the 'how' that is). You can consider this tone if one or more of the following scenarios are true:

- Business objectives are being met; however, the team seems to be set in their way and on autopilot instead of striving for improvement or excellence.

- It is harder to induct fresh blood into the team because of many manual, traditional or rudimentary processes and tools being used.

- People in your team are able to grow and thrive because of their tenure in the team or product, and not necessarily because of their skills and efforts.

- There are a lot of people dependencies, single points of failure, or bottlenecks in the team.

- People in your team often complain about uninteresting or boring day-to-day life.

- You want to foster the culture of learning and innovation in the team so that new ideas can come up.

- While there is no significant top-down push from leadership on your efficiency, you see that similar teams or competitors are able to produce the same or more output with fewer resources or in less time.

- You are looking to proactively find ways to continue to deliver the current accountability with fewer resources so that you can stake a claim on more by showing the spare capacity in your team.

In this case, you would be weaving your narrative to highlight the inside-out metrics like time spent on different activities and so on, instead of outside-in business metrics. The objective here will be to show the value of AI in making things faster, more convenient, or more polished. Here, the narrative will largely center around 'how' with the hint of 'so-what'.

Centered around survival

This case is neither about business goals nor about doing things better, but about the survival of the team or product in the mid to long-term, and where AI can be some kind of savior. The situation is dire and needs significant changes in order to be salvaged. A few of the scenarios where this can be a fitting narrative could be as follows:

- You were once a market leader, but the usage, popularity, or revenue is fast declining, and instead is siphoning off to a new competitor or an old one, who has cranked up the use of AI, resulting in an increase in their customer base.

- You are facing an acute attrition of your best employees, and lack of career growth and learning is one of the major factors the outgoing ones cite.

- Your team is unable to deliver on the ever-increasing expectations and business goals. The reasons holding them back are old processes, tools, or methods, and there are popular AI-fied cutting-edge options available in the market.

- You are finding it hard to attract good talent, and one of the major reasons seems to be that the technologies your team works on are considered outdated. There are better and more effective options available in the world, most prominently AI-based ones.

In this case, you would have to set up your narrative around your proposal to seize the slide and improve the situation in a meaningful way, and AI can be an obvious but major transformation that can help. The objective here is to propose a structured and data backed set of changes and steps that can revive the team, product or business from a rapidly degrading situation. Here, we should center the narrative mostly around 'how', with a supporting statement of 'why' and 'what'.

AI everywhere

This is the case where your proposal is not about simply meeting business goals or solving a set of problems in the team or product, but rather about promoting the use of as much AI everywhere as possible. The book suggests using this tone and building your story around this narrative in case one or more of the following scenarios are applicable:

- The leadership is pushing and championing the use of AI everywhere.

- On average, your team has been meeting business goals without AI.

- Your organization is settled, thriving and consists of motivated and highly productive members.

- Your objective is to push the envelope further and strive to make a larger impact and take on bigger things instead of being settled in the current steady state.

- You have a 'transformative' vision, which can be achieved with extensive use of AI.

- You want to set a benchmark for other teams or for the competition and want to leapfrog on the 'what' and 'how' of your business.

- Your leadership and organization are inviting and welcoming of innovative and transformative ways to build the future of the company or the product.

In this case, your narrative should focus on pitching and promoting the use of AI pretty much everywhere possible and look to paint an attractive and shiny future for everyone. The reference point of the story will not need to be the current state of the world and the changes AI will bring to it. Rather, we could simply paint the story of how the new world will look post-AI-fication. In other words, the story could look like one of starting from scratch and building the first version of a product or solution, as opposed to improvements in the current version. We can thus have complete freedom and not worry about carrying the baggage of the past. You will aim to build a very promising and hopeful story. In essence, your narrative will center a lot around the 'how' and relatively less around the 'what' and 'why'.

Deciding the narrative for leadership

As mentioned earlier, when thinking about the narrative, we suggest trying to put yourself in the leader's position and asking questions like:

- Why should we invest in something new?

- How will it benefit our company, business, or customers?

- What is the return on investment if we do this?

We should keep in mind that leaders might get a large number of proposals pitched every day, and while many of them would be really good and lucrative, the leaders cannot agree to all of them. They need some way to prioritize and pick the right ones. You can make it easier and quicker if your proposal does not oversell how good it is, but brings out the business impact clearly and prominently. In essence, the 'why', 'so-what', and 'what' might be more meaningful, and that too from the outside-in perspective, as opposed to the 'how'. We should couple this with the previously discussed tone and plot of the story, mission, and goal of the same, and then form the narrative keeping the 'what is in it' for the leadership.

We should also try to build in, as well as showcase to the leaders, that the plan consists of sufficient safety nets, checks and balances, and alternates in case things do not go according to plan. The narrative should also cover whether and what support and sponsorship you need from the leadership. Some of this might include additional resourcing for the transformation journey, access to the AI tools and resources, asking for evangelization of the plan from the leadership side to everyone, and so on.

Deciding the narrative for your team

Just like we approached the narrative for the leadership, for the narrative for our team, we should try to see this from the point of view of the team members. Some of the questions they might have could be on the lines of:

- Are we being asked to make changes because we are not doing something right, or are things not going well?

- Does the new method or technology affect my chances of learning and growth?

- Is this new technology coming here to replace me?

- What will happen if this new plan fails? Will I be penalized for that?

The narrative should try to ensure that the team feels supported, energized and aligned on the 'why' and 'what' from their perspective too, and not just expect them to go full throttle just because the organization or the manager is asking them to. Additionally, we should assure every team member, with the right supportive arguments, that this is a win-win direction and not lopsided towards what is coming from the top-down direction. The objective is to spend enough effort to garner genuine alignment and get everyone thoroughly excited and committed to the plan. Aligning them with mission, goals, benefits, and improved day-to-day life and future are some of the talking points that should be considered.

Establishing success criteria and metrics

There is a saying along the lines of: if it cannot be measured, it cannot be achieved. Essentially, it means that for any plan or goal, having a set of success criteria and measurable metrics or needles to move are super important to decide. We should decide those things before we embark on the journey so that we can assess the progress and direction on an ongoing basis and correct course or fail fast as soon as possible. We can do this in a few steps:

1. Once we have zeroed in on the plot and narrative of our story, the next step is to define the success criteria and metrics for the plan ahead. This will be essential to keeping track of progress and also for measuring success and its degree. These are also important to ensure that the specific work items, when created and assigned, can have a visible overarching theme, the 'what' and the 'why'.

2. We will weave these into 'goals' for the plan ahead. It is important to understand that here 'goals' is not necessarily referring to business goals but to the proposal or the AI transformation story forward which we are going to tell. There are a few examples we will present shortly to understand this better.

3. Next, we will define a mission statement. A mission statement is about the specific narrative we will pick regarding the plan of action and is not necessarily about something which relates to the company's business objectives. As we saw in the earlier sections of this chapter, whether or not these align only with business goals and objectives is a matter of the specific circumstances and aligns with the specific narrative we need to come up with.

Here are some of the sample goals and mission statements you can take inspiration from.

Case 1: Business objectives-based goals and mission

Mission statement: To be the trusted document indexing and search platform in the enterprise space.

Goal: Across the board, by the end of calendar year 2027, we would like to cut down our operating cost by 30% on average, while improving our monthly active users by 20%.

Case 2: Productivity and efficiency-based goals and mission

Mission statement: To be our organization's most efficient engineering team by adopting the most innovative technology, processes and tools.

Goals: By the end of this semester, we would like to be able to cut down our end-to-end development cycle by 25%. The two focus areas we would like to target are as follows:

- Time spent in testing a code change on average needs to be cut down from 6 hours to under 30 minutes.

- The 95th percentile time taken by code compilation is around 4 hours, and we would like to bring it to under 2 hours.

Once we have arrived at the goals and mission statements appropriate to our proposal, let us now look at how we will prepare the actual execution plan for the future.

Deciding changes for 30-60-90-days

As the last step in the preparation stage and before getting into execution mode, let us try to structure the items on the timeline to create a plan of execution. Typically, it is a good idea to bucketize them into short-term, mid-term, and long-term items. The definition of these will be specific to the overall timeline you have in mind.

Generally, for any meaningful and organization-wide effort, a quarter (3 months) is a reasonable timeframe to aim for. This period is not too short for the plan to have to bring in sudden and jarring changes and to be able to see meaningful impact. Similarly, this duration allows the room to change direction or stop without a lot of damage in case something was to go wrong without getting to a point of no return. Hence, keeping the 'long-term' to be 90-days in this case, let us assume short-term as 30-days and mid-term as 60-days.

Thinking about a 90-day period might still appear as being more tactical than being strategic in the larger scheme of things. Therefore, in the later chapters, the book will also provide suggestions and ideas on how to go about the longer-term period beyond these 90-days.

First 30-days

The best items to pick for the first 30-days would come from one or more of the following perspectives:

- Any preparatory tasks such as building design documents, mockups, and contracts between modules or teams. Having them upfront can help everyone focus on their own execution from this point onward. This will maximize the chances of multiple streams working in parallel, as they can be loosely coupled from this point on.

- The first set of easy wins and low-hanging fruits can be planned for this initial duration. This will help deliver value even though we are starting off and have not had time to make bigger changes. It will also help build early confidence about the plan and the hypothesis that went into it. Lastly, delivery always brings excitement, motivation, and accolades for the team, which can improve the morale, productivity, and energy of the team, which will also help get the best outcome for the next two milestones.

- Building more understanding of the possible unknowns of the overall plan by frontloading proof of concepts earlier in the journey around those. For instance, adopting AI will require us to try and see how the new AI tools or technologies perform in our specific use cases. This can be done best by incorporating those in a scaled-down subset of the product or process and seeing how it performs there.

- Building automated and self-sufficient ways to measure and report the metrics and numerical goals we had decided for the transformation should be targeted in this early period. This will help us get the capability of constantly keeping track of those going forward. This will also help us ensure that the goals we achieve are indeed measurable, and in case they are not, we are able to adjust the goals or explore alternate measurement techniques at the start itself, before we go too deep into execution.

- Similar to the previous point, building a testing framework and test cases upfront before we start developing the product or solution in question is a great thing to do. This will ensure that, as and when the features or improvements start to get built, we have the capability to validate their working from both functional and non-functional perspectives so that the team can keep moving to the next set of things. This will minimize the cases when we have to come back and revisit the previous work at a later point in time. This is sometimes also referred to as **test-driven development (TDD)** in the world of software engineering.

- Process-wise, it is good to establish how and at what frequency and format we will report and track the progress of the plan ahead, and also which data points will need to be provided by the team members to help with this on an ongoing basis. It will help to operate the plan much better and, again, help everyone to know their roles in execution as well as what parts of the process (such as the work item ticketing system) they need to keep updated.

Next 30-days

The middle phase of our execution plan is the most crucial one and should produce the highest amount and criticality of output. One reason for this is that the machinery is supposed to be past any starting trouble and in full swing. Moreover, we laid a good foundation in the first period of 30-days before entering this second period of 30-days. Hence, we should be able to make the fullest use of this period.

Some of the top themes and categories to consider for this phase are listed as follows:

- Schedule the tasks for implementing, testing, and completing the major parts of the various pieces that we designed, and for which we got the buy-off from the stakeholders in the previous phase.

- Plan for making early versions of the AI-fied products, solutions, and pipelines built so far, available to a limited internal audience and get early feedback. This will help validate whether they are on the lines of the originally agreed-upon mockups and specifications. Hence, schedule the tasks for internal drops, alpha testing and playing around with the early versions of the new artifacts, including time for fixing bugs or scheduling design and code changes, in case we need bigger fixes.

- Schedule the rhythm for regular gathering and reporting of various progress updates of the project for important stakeholders, such as the leadership. It is important to keep the 'investors' informed of how the work is progressing, and also if there are any changes that are coming to light, from the original plan, after the implementation phase has started.

- It is a great idea to plan for a few one-time early reviews and demos of the new world to the leadership and the team to build early excitement and get feedback.

- Towards the end of this second phase, it will be a good idea to decide and start to document the new rhythm of business, such as ways to work in the new world once you reach steady state, meetings and other collaboration you will need, as per the new paradigm, tools, processes or documentation you will need to create or alter and so on.

Last 30-days

The final phase of the execution plan is generally about closing, finalizing and giving finishing touches to the changes made. This is also the period when we close the door to the old world and transition to the shiny AI-fied new world.

Some of the top themes and tasks to consider in this phase could be as follows:

- Plan for getting a buy-off and, after that, putting the new business rhythm and other related things in place, which we discussed in the previous section, and retiring the old ones in a gradual but visible way.

- Plan a checkpoint at the start of this phase to assess the progress made relative to the original plan and whether things are playing out the same way or differently than we had originally imagined. This is a chance to learn and have time to make any course corrections, including thinking about plan B in case of major diversion.

- If the narrative was about incorporating AI in your product, plan the activities for releasing the beta or preview version of the product to customers in the early phase of this milestone. Towards the end of this milestone, plan for deploying the production version in a phased manner to all customers.

- Plan for a major review and demo with the leadership roughly around the middle of this phase to showcase the near final outcome of the plan and investments and get feedback which can be incorporated before we exit the overall 90-day transformation phase.

- Schedule an activity for building a plan which will cater to the longer-term steady state after this initial 90-day burst. This will include listing and planning for any further bigger changes that are needed based on what we learnt in this period. Moreover, as we have AI-fied a lot of things in the system, we will need to reassess the investments going forward. These are not necessarily about reducing the human capital because of AI but how differently things will operate now, and accordingly, the team will need to do a different set of things or work differently in the new world.

- It would be good to plan for a retrospective towards the end of this phase. This should cover looking back and gathering feedback on this 90-day 'sprint' from everyone as a closure and learning for the future.

- It will be crucial to plan for and schedule a set of planning exercises towards the end of this period or right after the 90-day period for the future ahead. We will need to make the call on how we will structure the way forward: do we need one or more similar 90-day transformation cycles after this, do we need a few monthly dashes from now on, or can we go back to a steadier state right after this of business as usual?

Conclusion

In this chapter, we connected all the dots we had gathered or built in the previous five chapters and used them to build a plan for the first major milestone of a quarter towards the transformation into the new AI-enabled world. We also touched on the importance of storytelling, measurable goals, mission statements, and building narratives for various segments of the organization via storytelling. Going forward, we will focus on how to put this plan in motion and where do we go from there.

In the next chapter, we will look at the execution phase where we will discuss how to put the plan we built in this chapter into action. We will also learn some of the best practices and steps to achieve execution excellence.

Join our Discord space

Join our Discord workspace for latest updates, offers, tech happenings around the world, new releases, and sessions with the authors:

https://discord.bpbonline.com

CHAPTER 7
Execute the Transformation

Introduction

In the previous chapter, which was the first phase of our AI transformation journey, we worked on creating a 90-days plan for the initial burst. In this chapter, we will discuss the second phase of the AI journey: execution. While a great plan is crucial for such a large-scale and high-stakes transformational journey, the plan can only be fruitful if the execution is up to the mark, to follow that excellent plan! As the saying goes, the best ideas or plans can fail without good execution, and great execution can make an average idea really shine. We will look at some of the key tips for great execution in general, with a special focus on the 30-60-90-days period.

Structure

This chapter covers the following topics:

- Tips for moving from planning to execution
- Reviewing and questioning the how and the what

- Ongoing retrospectives to fine-tune the approach

Objectives

We will take the narrative, goals, mission statement, and the 30-60-90-days execution plan we built in the previous chapter and discuss how to put all of them into action in the best way possible. As before, we will look at this in a generic way and work out a template of sorts, which you can apply, depending on your specific narrative, goals, and situation, and have your own version of the perfect execution.

Tips for moving from planning to execution

In the book so far, we have spent extensive efforts in gathering all the ingredients, setting wheels in motion, coming up with goals, a mission, tailored narratives, and closing with the short-term, mid-term, and long-term execution plans. There was a lot of thinking, analysis, and theorizing involved. Now, we will get into the more practical aspects in order to get them going. Here are some of the considerations for putting each of these into practice.

Pitching the story to leadership

In the previous chapter, we dived deep into preparing a compelling proposal for the members of the leadership. We carefully tailored our tone, crux, and metrics based on the specific circumstances and kind of AI transformation that the team and the organization need. The hard work we had put into doing that should be nearly sufficient for getting an alignment and obtaining their approval to move ahead with the plan. Here are a few other things to consider while delivering the pitch, in order to land the necessary impact:

- Ensure that your confidence and conviction in the plan come out well. This can be infectious and help the leadership feel good to kick things off.

- Ensure that the centerpiece of the plan is reemphasized and clear: whether it is business metrics or an ambitious AI revolution. This helps reestablish alignment and goals before starting execution.

- If there is any adjustment to the existing deliverables you have to give because you are taking this transformation up, it is good to explicitly get acknowledgement and support from the leadership about the same.

Pitching the story to the team

We took a thorough effort to compile the best narrative for the team members, as well as in the previous chapter, to establish alignment and agreement with them. It is important to note that alignment is not permanent and needs repeated affirmation and check-in frequently. More so, the start of the first phase of execution, before the day-to-day work itself, will play a big part in consistently staying aligned. Some of the points to consider when pitching the story to your team members are as follows:

- Ensure that you spend the extra effort to approach each team member individually and tailor your pitch for each of them. This should include talking about the upside they personally will see both as part of the journey and as an outcome of this transformation.

- In a clear but subtle manner, establish the expectations for the upcoming 90-day period and for each of the phases, as they differ slightly. One obvious expectation to set is that everyone understands this is a dash and hence ensures that they are at their best and most efficient.

- Normally, the success criteria of the task they will be doing are considered the same as the success criteria for the individual's performance. However, it is important to decouple the two and discuss with the team member about the 'how' of the task being crucial, as well as for their success. We should ensure that they would not try just to complete the task, but also do it in the best way possible.

- Re-emphasize to the team the notion of a shared mission and shared success. It is good to note that the organization and leadership are counting on and investing in them for entering the next AI phase by doing this 90-day dash with all of their efforts.

Estimation of each task before starting the first 30-days

As they say, well begun is half done. Hence, getting to a good start of the transformation is a fundamental goal to target. To make this possible, we should start by doing an accurate estimation of the work items that we identified for the first 30-day period in the previous chapter. It is a good strategy to do this together as a team, and thus take inputs from everyone for a more grounded estimation. While doing the estimation, one thing that helps get them right is not to assume which individual will be working on what task, thus keeping the estimation generic. Additionally, as the manager, you should review the initial estimations for accuracy and make any adjustments, as needed, before moving forward.

Increasing confidence by incorporating a buffer

Adding some buffer to the estimation in the proportion of the number of unknowns for that task will be a good strategy. The higher the number of unknown factors the task contains, the higher the possibility of the estimation being inaccurate, and hence the higher amount of buffer should be accounted for, and vice versa. Typically, the range of buffer percent could be anywhere from 10% to as high as 50%. By doing this, we will be able to increase the confidence and probability of the execution being as close as possible to the plan. This will help prevent slips or surprises later in the cycle and also minimize the ripple effect on the rest of the plan. When dealing with cutting-edge technology, the number of unknowns might be high, and hence, it will be good to add a somewhat higher buffer to those tasks that involve doing something using the new AI technology and tools.

Sequencing of tasks

After coming up with estimations for the tasks pertaining to the first 30-days, we should next try to divide those tasks into each of the 4 weeks of this 30-day period and decide which of the tasks will be planned for which of the weeks. There are many well-known and established aspects of execution to consider, such as accounting for dependencies, the amount of parallel execution possible, and so on. The same applies to the AI transformation journey as well, and we should apply it when sequencing and laying out the tasks for each of the weeks.

Assignment of tasks to the right team members

It is important to consider the right match of a task to a corresponding team member. This, in accordance with the right estimation and the right amount of buffer, increases the confidence level and chances of success of the task. It also helps to weave in the right kind of challenges and learnings for each team member according to their needs and wants, as per their career stage. This will also improve the quality of the task because the person working on it is highly motivated and sees value in doing it for their benefit as well. It is also helpful to involve the team in doing these assignments to ensure their inputs and preferences are also considered.

We can see a few examples here:

- If the task consists of predictable and straightforward work and fewer unknowns to solve for, it is possibly best to assign it to the team member who has not yet perfected and learned excellent execution and delivery skills.

- The tasks that require more coordination and collaboration with one or more stakeholders are possibly ideal for someone who possesses them as their key strengths.

- The tasks that are the most ambiguous and have a large amount of complexity and unknowns are best assigned to those team members who are seasoned and will be well-served with such a challenge and opportunity.

We should note that it is not always possible to get to the perfect match because it depends on the nature of the overall list of tasks and the team's composition. The book recommends finding the best possible match in the given circumstances or constraints, and moving forward with that.

Adjusting the estimates once more before starting

It should be noted that after doing the assignment, it is a good idea to revisit the estimation and buffering once more, in order to make any minor adjustments necessary. This is also important because, as we mentioned before, we might not always end up with the perfect assignments possible. Here are some examples to consider:

- If a complex task is assigned to someone for whom it will result in a higher learning curve, then we may want to add a further buffer than what we had originally added.

- In case a task is picked up by someone who is an expert in that area or technology and a seasoned person, and they might need a lesser-than-average amount of time to do the task, then the estimation and buffers can be reduced for that task.

As a conclusion, it is good to validate that the estimation is right for the specific person who is picking up that task.

Re-evaluating the trajectory for the next 30-days

Many of the considerations, such as estimation and task assignment, which we discussed for the first 30-day period, will apply to this period as well. However, there are a few additional things to consider. By the end of the first 30-day period, we will have a good amount of data to assess the velocity of execution and accuracy of our original estimations, based on how the execution really turned out. Depending upon this, for the next 30-day period, it will be good to adjust the estimations and buffer amounts accordingly. This will help readjust the trajectory of progress going forward.

Here are two of the most likely scenarios:

- If many of the tasks were completed faster than planned, it would be good to be a bit more positive and aggressive. Hence, we can reduce the estimations or buffers for the remaining tasks.

- If the tasks took longer than expected due to unanticipated or unknown factors, higher than expected complexity, or inaccurate dependency factors, it will be good to increase the estimations or buffers accordingly for the next 30-day period.

Revisiting the assignments for the second phase

In addition to the trajectory, it is also a good opportunity to revisit the task assignments. In the first 30-day period, it is possible that certain team members were able to breeze through work faster than expected. You can choose to give them higher complexity tasks than before, if there is scope to do that. Similarly, there might be certain team members who find it harder to deal with the unknowns that come with shiny new AI tools and technology. We can give them more time and help than before, and adjust the estimation or assignments accordingly. Making these adjustments will ensure a win-win scenario both for the execution as well as for the team members.

Thinking about the last 30-days

Similar to the middle period of 30-days, we should adjust the various aspects of the trajectory and assignments while entering the last 30-day period as well. Hopefully, the changes will be minimal, given that we would have gotten more accurate execution of our plans by now.

In addition to that, the last period of 30-days is highly critical to the overall completion of the dash. While a good beginning is essential, nothing matters more than an excellent finish. Hence, it will be good to gather the team around and discuss the same. We should revalidate and repose the shared mission we started off with, and we also need one last push to ensure success. This might need a bit more 'extra' from everyone to keep the schedule and quality on target. Finding ways to decide and communicate any incentives and winding down events that you will do after this dash will be a great idea and motivation for the team members.

Reviewing and questioning the 'how' and 'what'

One of the important aspects of excelling in execution is to keep a close watch on the micro milestones as well. Within that, not just focus on the outcome (the 'what') but also the way the micro-steps are being planned and executed (the 'how'). AI transformation can be very tricky since we are likely challenging decades of practices and habits as well as trying to change them in a big and fundamental way. Hence, it is important to have a cautiously optimistic approach when executing this 90-day dash.

Defining intermittent milestones

The organic thing we did in the previous chapter and early part of this chapter was to divide the overall work (the 'how') into weekly and monthly parts, for best possible execution. In addition to that, it is good to identify a few top-down, as well as bottoms-up milestones (the 'what') in this journey. The easiest way is to pick the top-level metrics we had defined for this transformation and see how much they have moved after each of the 2 weeks period. It is good to announce and celebrate these interim victories, to motivate and validate the team's efforts and the fact that they are producing results.

Keeping the progression of 'what' in view

Now that we have defined the intermittent logical milestones, it goes without saying that you as the leader of the transformation, should keep a close watch on this (the 'what'). You should share the progress and completions via announcements and as part of formal or informal team meetings and leadership forums. The frequency and format of such updates should be crisp, consistent, and interesting. If the progression of these metrics is not in proportion to the time elapsed in this journey, it is good to re-pivot as soon as possible, instead of letting the plan flow as originally decided.

Keeping the 'how' going right

The 'how' of the transformation is represented by the list of work items we have created. We should keep a close watch on them being executed well. This includes measuring if the amount of remaining work is roughly proportionate to the time elapsed, and also that the estimations are holding true when the real execution is being done. A fitting set of forums to do this can be the frequent team huddles. A suitable frequency of such huddles (or 'scrum' as we also call them) in our case could be daily or at a minimum of 3 times a week.

An appropriate set of questions to find answers in these stand-ups could be as follows:

- For a given task and by each person, what progress has been made since the last huddle?

- What specifically is the person looking to complete in the next 1 or 2-days?

- Does the person need any help?

- Are there any blockers or dependencies preventing anyone from making some forward progress?

Being A(I)-gile

It should also be noted that the world of AI is rapidly evolving and can be an important factor, external to our plan, which needs to be considered on a regular basis. Even a period of 90-days can be long from this perspective, where newer models, tools, and data might have emerged since the time we laid the plan out. In fact, that is one of the reasons the book previously referred to even a 90-day period as 'long-term'. At the same time, it is unlikely that within this period your plans will become completely irrelevant due to the change of the AI world.

Hence, in the execution phase, it is good to constantly stay up-to-date with newer or better versions of AI tech being released or perfected. Examples of this could be the introduction of newer AI models that are performing better than the previous ones or a brand-new tool that is superior for a task as compared to the previous one. Thus, the book recommends fine-tuning or tweaking the 'how' as a result of this.

It might look like this will slow down the process. But in fact, in the larger scheme of things, owing to using a better solution than before, you might be able to complete the work faster, and hence the change in direction mid-way will in fact turn out to be a time saver. Moreover, doing this makes your solution and processes much more in tune with the rest of the world as opposed to having to redo some work later to catch up.

Reviews with leadership

As discussed in the previous chapter, we had planned for reviews with leadership at various checkpoints. These reviews can serve as an excellent forcing function and source of evaluating and learning the progress in an objective manner. These will also be extremely helpful in getting important encouragement and feedback from the leadership. In the previous chapter, we already covered the recommended timings of these reviews and discussed the topics and narratives to be covered in them. Here are some of the things to consider while conducting these reviews:

- These reviews are a good place to thank the leadership for their support and sponsorship. We should also use this opportunity to highlight the team's collaboration and contributions.

- Consider approaching each of these intermittent reviews as a self-contained story instead of assuming everyone already knows what you are trying to do in the transformation overall.

- Use the metrics decided in the beginning to weave your narrative about the progress made and current status.

- The story can be based on one or more of the following points:

    o Let us recall and start with our purpose, objective and success criteria we had agreed on before starting this journey.

    o We are at this particular juncture (example: 1/3rd of the way) of the overall AI transformation journey. Let us review the progress and outcomes we have achieved so far, as compared to where we had expected to have reached by now.

- o The execution so far has mostly been as planned, and we are on track to achieve our transformation goals by the end of this 90-day dash.

  or

- o We have run into some unforeseen glitches and hence our plan is only 60% successful so far. We have made adjustments to the plan and brought down our goals by 20%, which can be achieved within this 90-day period.

- In case the execution is off track, be prepared to answer what, if anything, it will take to bring it back on track. It could be things like $x\%$ more resources, a different technology and so on.

- If things are going better than planned, be prepared to propose what you would like to change for the rest of the 90-day tenure. It could be upping the goals, reducing the number of resources you need, or taking on another set of goals as well.

- The leadership is generally also interested in applying the template and learnings coming from one of the teams to the other part of the organization. This helps with the betterment of the organization at large and also reduces the need for multiple teams to reinvent the wheel. It will be a good idea to prepare at least a high-level abstract template and narrative, which, if needed, can be taken up by another team or for another problem space.

How of the 'how'

The double use of 'how' here is to disambiguate the list of tasks (the 'how') from how the team members are doing them. Most of the time, there are multiple ways to do the same thing. One can do the task in the straightforward way as they have always done, or find a better, more efficient and more intelligent way of doing it. In our case, our higher-order objective was to move to a more AI-integrated world. Therefore, we should ensure that the team members are incorporating more AI-enabled and efficient ways into their work. Thus, a positive side effect of doing the task will be that the journey of evolving our habits to use more AI will start early.

Let us take an example of one of the tasks, that is, generating the test cases in the beginning for the aforementioned **test-driven development** (TDD). In a steady state, we would consider this to be an obvious partial or complete use case of available AI tools. However, instead of waiting for the 90-day transformation to be over, this itself is an ideal opportunity to learn and use the appropriate AI tool to generate or fine-tune the test cases.

Early customer feedback

In the previous chapter, we discussed providing an early-stage preview of our AI-fied product or solution to a select set of customers and stakeholders. It is an essential input in this journey taken at the appropriate time when things are just about ready for an external view, as well as not too late to make changes. As discussed earlier, we should do this at least a couple of times in this journey to not only take feedback but also validate that things are on track and will be accepted by the customers when we finally release them in production.

Here are some of the key things to consider in this effort:

- Selection of customers for this effort is an important ingredient for maximizing the chances of success. Apart from ensuring that the selected set is trustworthy and credible, we should pick a mix of customers in different stages of their journey. Some early AI enthusiasts, some well-settled and pragmatic ones, and some of those who are happy and satisfied with the current state of the world will help us get a full 360-degree perspective.

- The speed of turnaround is very critical in this 90-day dash. Hence, it will be good not just to hand the customers the under-construction version of the product but also to engage with them more closely. We should assign one or more team members to work closely with a customer to get to try the product out and experience the journey first-hand.

- As discussed in another context earlier, when dealing with humans for anything, it is a good idea to think about how to incentivize and motivate them to do something. The opportunity for trying out the latest AI-fied version of your product or solution seems like a pretty appealing one, but it is seldom sufficient to get things going. We recommend preparing a mini-pitch for the customers we picked for this trial to incentivize them to help. Here are some of the possible talking points:

- o We offer you an excellent opportunity to play with the most cutting-edge technology that others in the industry have not yet seen.

- o You have a fantastic opportunity to help shape the future of your beloved product. Not only that, you will experience a white-glove treatment where we will be closely listening to you and incorporating your questions and feedback, which you will later benefit from!

- o This is a rare opportunity to interact directly with the team that works on building products and solutions that your business benefits from. You can impart your points of view directly to them so they can carry those forward for the future as well.

- Similar to the customers, we should also address our team members who we are asking to spend time with customers, for running these trials and gathering feedback. Some of the possible talking points to consider are as follows:

  - o It is one of the rare opportunities that you, as the developer of the product or solution, get to see it being used in real life. The satisfaction of seeing your work in action, helping a customer solve a problem, is extremely rewarding.

  - o You have the rare opportunity to directly influence the direction of our short-term or long-term roadmap and priorities, which otherwise are always considered to come top-down.

  - o You get to put yourself in the customer's shoes and find use cases for yourself as well for the product you have helped build.

Ongoing retrospectives to fine-tune the approach

As the undertaking is full of unknowns and major changes, keeping a growth mindset and an approach of quick learning and pivoting will be extremely helpful. The book suggests taking an approach of doing retrospectives, both on-the-spot and planned ones, after the end of each mini-milestone.

It should be noted that there might be some important new work items that might emerge from this analysis. We should make room for and schedule a few of them in the remaining part of the 90-day period, depending on their criticality. It might be fine to schedule some of them for a later time, too, if the return on investment on doing them right away does not impact the scope of the 90-day dash.

Let us have a closer look at some of the strategies and methodologies for doing retrospectives.

On-the-spot retrospectives

Given that we are dealing with a fast-paced 90-day dash, each day and each event is worth deep-diving soon after it happens. Hence, in case there are any new revelations, failures, or hiccups seen, we recommend doing a retrospective fairly soon, maybe right after the situation is resolved. We should note that the tone and goal of these retrospectives should be objective, and to learn more and fix things going forward. Hence, this act should not come across as looking for the person to hold responsible for the failure.

This activity is also known as **root cause analysis (RCA)** or, at times, as **postmortem**. Getting to the root of the issue or situation and identifying what we will do to make sure the same or similar thing does not happen again is extremely important. One of the ways to do an effective RCA is to ask the 5-whys, meaning, asking the 'w' questions 5 times to uncover one layer of the issue each time. The questions we should try to find answers to are on the lines of the following:

- What really happened?

- What was the impact of this?

- How did we overcome the situation?

- What could have prevented this in the first place?

- What can we put in place or change so that this does not happen again?

We should make sure to use a template and a repository for documenting and storing these for future reference. This will also help pass the learnings to broader teams or organizations that might not have been involved in the event or fixing of the same. Doing this might benefit them so that they themselves can prevent something similar from happening in their world.

Recurring retrospectives

This is the set of retrospectives that are more generic and not specific to one particular event or issue. These can be scheduled at the end of each week or 2 week periods, depending upon the pace and size of the team. The larger the team, the better it is to convene at shorter durations to ensure we do not drift away quickly. The retrospectives are also known as **retro ceremony** in large parts of the engineering industry.

Unlike the on-the-spot retrospectives, the objective of the regular retrospectives is not to fix or root cause an issue or a problem, but rather, to take a holistic stock of the execution on the ground. Therefore, this will involve the entire team and not just a specific set of people. In addition, this will generally include finding answers to the following questions:

- What went well?

- What did not go well?

- What should we 'continue doing' or do more of?

- What should we 'stop' doing?

- What should we 'start' doing?

Here, too, it will be good to use a shared platform, where every team member can post their own answers, preferably anonymously, and all other team members should be able to read them. You can also choose someone other than you, the manager, to run this ceremony and collate the responses. Unless the team needs to do otherwise, the retrospective document might be good to confine to within the team instead of sharing broadly.

We should encourage the team to spend time not only reporting the previously mentioned answers but also deciding on actionable steps they would like to recommend the team take to improve or sustain the situation. These retrospectives are also a good opportunity to pass on acknowledgements of great individual or team accomplishments and to thank them. It might also be a good idea to increase the high-level observations and takeaways coming out of these retrospectives with the leadership. These can be shared as part of the reviews we will do with leadership, as mentioned in the earlier pages of this chapter.

Retrospective for planning

We discussed the two retrospectives that are done during the 90-day journey. The book recommends another, more of a big picture retrospective spanning the entire 90-day transformation. The suggestion is to look back at the entire journey together as a team, where you can optionally include a select set of leadership members, too. The objective of doing so is to review the overall approach and process for learning and future improvements.

Here are some of the questions we should try to find answers to:

- How useful and effective was our planning cycle and process? In retrospect, what are the changes you would suggest making for the planning to be more effective?

- In retrospect, how was our estimation process and methodology? Knowing what we know now, are there any additional factors we should have considered while estimating?

- How useful did each of the team members find the learning and challenges? Did we have sufficient room for making mistakes and learning?

- Did the journey feel collaborative and constructive, or was there room for improvement?

Conclusion

In this chapter, we learnt how to turn our AI transformation plan into reality by striving for execution excellence. We discussed nuances and different focus areas pertaining to each phase and the stakeholders involved in achieving the best possible outcomes. This should help to prepare the reader for going about their own AI transformation with confidence and conviction.

This concludes our one-time dash to bring about major AI transformation in the team. In the remaining chapters of this book, we will cover some more ideas to bring about more long-lasting and permanent AI orientation in the team. The next chapter kicks it off with the topic of learning from the 90-day dash and planning forward as the bridge between the short-term dash and the long-term vision.

Join our Discord space

Join our Discord workspace for latest updates, offers, tech happenings around the world, new releases, and sessions with the authors:

https://discord.bpbonline.com

CHAPTER 8
Feedback Loop

Introduction

In the previous two chapters, we went on a 90-day dash to bring about a major one-time AI-enabled transformation to our team, product, solutions, and processes. The current chapter aims to serve as the bridge between the short-term dash and the long-term AI-fied future. We would additionally suggest that a major transformation like this will need some more time to completely fall into place, and the next 90-day period is an important timeframe for ensuring that happens. In this chapter, we will look at some ideas of how to enable the listening and feedback system, to help get the pulse of various key stakeholders and use this to make big or small changes for the follow-up period.

Structure

This chapter covers the following topics:

- Setting up listening and feedback channels

- Keeping room for dialogue and changes
- Keeping an ear to the ground on advancements in AI

Objectives

This chapter will cover the journey of the next 90-day period and things to consider for this period for the team, product, and process. We will discuss how to seamlessly get back to steady state, following the 90-day dash while keeping the essence of the changed approach, coming from the AI transformation it brought. We will also discuss the importance and methodology of setting up the feedback loop and how to incorporate this feedback into planning and execution. Lastly, we will also try to learn some ideas on how to get plugged into advancements in AI. This will be crucial for our long-term strategy and will be an important piece we utilize in the rest of the book.

Setting up listening and feedback channels

Right after having gone through a 90-day dash to turn the ship by a large degree and point it towards the AI-fied world, now is the time to enable the signals for assessing progress and direction. This is an important step, especially in the period that directly follows the 90-day dash, as it is our last chance to make any changes before things become permanent. The very first thing for us to get started on should be setting up various channels for getting feedback. Note that some of these might already exist in your system. In that case, the activity turns into polishing and increasing attention towards them. Let us now look at four important avenues for us to plug in, namely the customers, leadership, the team, and the compete. Some of these can continue beyond the 90-day period as well for continued learning and improvements.

Customers

It is needless to say that customers are the most important element of the product and solution ecosystem, because they are the reason why we build what we build. Hence, we should find the best and fastest channels for customers to provide us feedback and for us to be able to consume it easily. Without going into comprehensive details of this, here are some of the considerations and dimensions to look for:

- Consider building mechanisms in the product or solution for customers to provide 'in-context' feedback or issues when they use a new feature or enhancement. For our AI transformation and for these 90-days, it might be a good idea to increase them a bit more around the areas which we changed, and we need to learn how customers are perceiving those.

- Consider building an automated pipeline to connect the customer-reported issue or feedback to it getting stored, with relevant context and being easy to retrieve and process later.

- Consider building a mechanism for the customer to report overall experience and satisfaction with the product or solution, sometimes also referred to as **customer satisfaction** (**CSAT**). This could be a numerical score that the customer can provide, say on a scale of 1 to 5. Additionally, we should have a way for them to also provide textual comments to elaborate on anything they want to call out.

- We should have automated mechanisms to aggregate these scores, as well as plot their trends to see if things are improving or degrading, with the ongoing changes we made to the product or solution. For textual comments, we should consider building a sentiment analysis kind of system, so we can extract the gist of the feedback without having to go through each and every word provided by each customer.

- Lastly, as we are talking about AI, it will be useful to utilize AI for this. We can put in place an AI-based mechanism to analyze both the CSAT trends and the textual feedback and come up with the insights and recommendations. This will save a lot of manual time to go through a large amount of feedback and also to decide what the feedback is saying and what actions we should take. Depending upon the nature of your business, you should also integrate it with social media channels to tap into the relevant posts and #tags, and so on.

Leadership

Next, after the customers, we should find ways to ensure we gather feedback from leadership quickly and clearly during this 90-day period. This feedback is likely to encompass business, market, company direction, and customer voice, which the leaders might have heard. Hence, this can be a great source of actionable tasks and set us up for success. There are many tried and tested ways to gather this feedback, and we will summarize a few thoughts here without getting into comprehensive details:

- We should make our key leaders proactively aware that certain parts of the product, solution or process are on an AI-fication journey, and they should keep a watch on things coming up pertaining to those surfaces. Moreover, encourage them to try those things themselves as well to provide their first-hand perspectives too!

- Share the customer feedback and actionable plan with them and seek validation or input. You can do this using periodic offline updates via email or newsletters.

- Encourage them to periodically and proactively share guidance and directions, especially in this 90-day period, for a faster turnaround.

- While not strictly related to the feedback aspect, we can also take this opportunity to appraise the leadership to attend to any negative publicity about the new changes made, which potentially might arise. Depending upon the specifics, they would need to de-escalate some of it, educate the world about why the changes were on the right path or bring those back to the product group as something which they should fix.

Team

The two channels we talked about so far will help us get valuable outside-in feedback. Let us now talk about inside-out or bottom-up feedback as well, that is, coming from our team. We had kept the team engaged throughout this journey and also had shown them the specific benefits of the AI transformation we are asking them to participate in. Now, it will be important to reverse the direction of the information flow and see how things are really panning out.

Additionally, our three personas will also have something to say after all the action we have taken them through. Here are a few of the considerations for the best results:

- We recommend conducting a few listening sessions and team huddles where you can bring up the goals and promises we have started off with, show the impact and progress, and seek their input and opinions. This will also help refresh their memory and realign them with the mission.

- Utilize 1:1s with them to assess if the individual is seeing their efficiency and effectiveness improve with the changes that we brought in using AI. Check if they feel that they have learned new tools and skills in the process, as promised earlier, and feel good about their career and growth as a result.

- Out of the three personas we discussed earlier, empower and encourage especially the Type B and C team members to provide their views on positives and negatives they might be experiencing with the transformation we have undertaken. Moreover, encourage them to continue to find time to keep learning and trying out the advancements in the AI world and bring back any recommendations or improvements they can come up with.

Compete

Competitors are an important factor in what we do, and we should keep a close watch on how they are evolving and bringing 'what' or 'how' changes in the wake of AI. Please note that it is impossible to engage with them to get this information or feedback directly. Hence, this avenue is different from the other three we discussed so far, in that obtaining feedback from this one will not be straightforward. Here are a few considerations and recommendations for this particular channel of feedback:

- Use publicly available information to learn how your top two or three competitors have been dealing with the AI evolution.

- Generally, there are many independent entities that are running a compete analysis in order to help customers choose the best solution. It is good to learn about those and tap into the data and analysis they are providing, especially to learn the effect of our AI-fication done in the 90-day dash.

- Wherever legally possible, we can also set up an ongoing side-by-side comparison mechanism to learn first-hand about the standings on critical metrics and experiences.

- We will also generally learn from customers, as well as part of their feedback or direction, in case they have better offerings coming from a competitor, and extract that information for our consumption as well.

Keeping room for dialogue and changes

Earlier in this chapter, we worked on establishing listening channels and a feedback loop. We also need to have a mechanism to utilize all the inputs coming from those and act on them. In addition, we should find ways to keep room in our plan for both analyzing this feedback as well as changing the course of action midway if needed, based on it. Next, in this chapter, we will discuss a few considerations and dimensions of going about the same.

Making use of the incoming feedback

In the previous section, we established new feedback channels and amplified the existing ones. In the day-to-day work, it is essential to find seamless ways to incorporate and utilize that feedback and make real changes and improve things based on it. The book recommends especially focusing on doing this in the 90-day period directly following the 90-day dash, more so than what one would do in the steady state. Next, we will look at each of the types of feedback and how to weave them into our scheme of things for this 90-day period.

Feedback from customers

As we mentioned earlier, customers are generally the main reason we do what we do. In terms of priority of all the feedback, customer feedback, especially when we are in the relatively early phase in the AI-fication journey, is extremely important to pay attention to. This feedback will be a direct early indication of whether or not our plan is on the right track. The following are some of the steps and ideas to take action on this feedback:

1. Set up a regular rhythm of reviewing this feedback and creating work items out of the accepted ones, also known as **triage**. A good frequency of doing this could be twice a week or weekly, depending on the size of the customer base and the volume of the feedback. You can include a selected set of team members to participate in this exercise.

2. Device or decide on a framework to prioritize and categorize the feedback. The goal is to decide how important this input is, relative to the rest of the work we already have scheduled within this 90-day period, and also to decide when to schedule this particular work item amongst them. There are many well-known frameworks available, such as **reach, impact, confidence, and effort (RICE), must have, should have, could have, and won't have (MoSCoW),** Kano Model and so on. The main essence and purpose of all of them is to do a cost-benefit analysis of the feedback and the corresponding work item.

3. Schedule these work items accordingly in the corresponding week, in this 90-day period, amongst the rest of the work. This might mean some lower priority items will move to later in this period or completely out of the 90-day period, and that is the right thing to do.

4. Decide and establish when and which release each of these selected improvements will be delivered to the customer in. If possible, create a theme around multiple of these, to create a meaningful update or major release for the customer, which makes it worth for them to take up this update.

Feedback from leadership

Leadership feedback is crucial and, many times, binding as well. It is important to take this on face value and with utmost importance, because most of the time, this is a good representation of the customer, market, as well as company dynamics and situation. Here are a few things to consider with respect to this feedback channel:

- We recommend having a dialogue with the leadership when feedback is received, instead of dropping everything and trying to address it. It is good to seek clarity and more details from them if they think this is a must-do, good to do, or merely a suggestion.

- It is also good to ask the 'why' question and discuss which success metrics pertaining to the business or customers will benefit from this reason.

- According to the priority agreed on, we should inject the feedback from the leadership into the current stream of execution and make way for it, or plan for these as future improvements for later.

Feedback from the team

A big part of bringing AI into the mix is to modify the 'how' of things. Hence, it is important to have the opportunity and mechanism for the technical experts to help bring up changes and improvements in a frictionless manner, more so in this 90-day period. This will help smooth our transition a bit more, as well as keep us in tune with technical advancements as much as possible. The following are some of the recommendations and steps we can take in this regard:

- Recommend that the AI experts of your team also keep a watch on any inputs coming from the team members. Encourage them also to check in with them frequently and learn if there are any challenges being faced by them or if there are any other suggestions.

- Review their feedback and suggestions regularly. We recommend closing the loop with them, for each of their suggestions, to convey whether you plan to incorporate the change, not consider it, or park for later.

- We recommend using a prioritization framework to determine the cost-benefit of the major suggestions. This helps prioritize the bottoms-up suggestions not only from the 'how' angle but also makes it easier to slot it amongst the rest of the business goals and customer asks.

Feedback from compete analysis

One of the feedback channels we had established in the previous section was to keep an eye on what our major competitors are doing. There might be a temptation to react to this and keep changing our direction all the time. However, the book recommends putting this into perspective in the bigger picture and with the rest of the factors, rather than simply looking to mimic or follow the competition. The following are some of the considerations and actions that we will recommend pertaining to this channel of feedback:

- It is good to assess whether this item is also showing up in some way in the feedback from the customer channel. We also recommend consulting with leadership or checking if this was also part of their feedback. For example:

  o It is possible that the new feature our top competitor has released is something the customer cares about or wants the most. In that case, we should also try to prioritize it soon to close the gap between us and the competitor's offering.

  o It is possible that the competitor is playing to their strengths and looking to change the game instead of solving the problems the customers really have. Based on this, we would recommend that you either decide to change course or ignore the move from your competitor for now.

- Many times, there are optics associated with such improvements that we should pay attention to. For example, if the competitor is advertising something like 'we are running on the most cutting-edge version of the model', it is possible that many customers would gravitate towards them. You can decide to do something about plugging this gap in the competitive advantage with them. The solution might be simply to scramble and move to the newer model yourself, or publish a study or test results on why the new model is not the one the customers need, and stay on the existing version.

- Remember that for your competitors, you are the competitor, and they are also thinking and doing similar things. Hence, it will be good to make an informed decision about whether you are the leader anyway. In the market, you know that the competition is doing it for their survival in this highly competitive environment, and accordingly, you can consider those changes as of lower importance and park them for later.

Evolution of goals and success measures

In the steady state, we are largely driven by a set of business goals as the guiding factor to determine the direction and measure success. In the previous two chapters, we had come up with a set of goals and success measures for the AI transformation as an input to the 90-day dash. We recommend leveraging that crucial effort a bit further and factoring these new measures in when going about the next 90-day period.

Some of the advantages of doing this could be as follows:

- This will give the team and product the opportunity to complete any spillover work items coming out of the 90-day dash and perfect the system.

- This will also help in having another iteration of fine-tuning and adjustments for any new developments in the world of AI.

- Last but not least, you will need to ensure to prioritize addressing major feedback coming from our first AI-fied customer release done at the end of the 90-day dash.

Agility in planning

For the 90-day dash, the book emphasized the importance of doing rigorous and meticulous planning for the entire 90-day period. This included deciding on work items for each of the weeks in this period in advance. While we had the recommendation of making tweaks as per how the execution had gone up to that particular point in time, we still assumed we would make minimal changes to the original plan. The objective was to keep us focused on making as much forward progress as possible and steer the ship in the direction of having AI as the way of life. Moreover, the goal was to make sure to build living proof of the benefits of AI for customers, as well as showcase that business metrics are moving as well.

In the 90-day period directly following the dash, it will make more sense for the approach to planning to become more Agile. We recommend bringing in a good mix of being proactive as well as reactive, instead of planning too far ahead and planning for the entire 90-day period together. As mentioned in the customer feedback section earlier, we can choose one of the prioritization frameworks to fairly and objectively prioritize various goals and work items. Here are some of the points to consider to put this in practice:

- Plan for the goals and metrics (the 'what') one month at a time instead of the complete 90-day period. This will ensure that the commitment and focus of the team are kept and that the execution is still steered in a deterministic direction.

- As covered in the previous sections, the recommendation is that these goals should consist of a mix of both the business goals (the outside-in) as well as the ones related to the 'how' itself (the inside-out).

- Each month, we recommend laying out the list of tasks (the 'how') for achieving the monthly goal. However, we should do this at a high-level instead of spending time going too deep and granular at the start.

- During the 90-day dash, we had planned for frequent and recurring checkpoints, announcements and reviews with the leadership and stakeholders based on time elapsed. In the next period of 90-days, we should change this to do on an as-needed basis, essentially when we have a meaningful update to share, instead of sharing something every 2 weeks or every month. This is the same approach we also do when we are in a steady state phase, where we do not overcommunicate the fact that we are making progress. Instead, we would share things as and when we have something important enough for them to pay attention to.

- Similar to the previous point, the previews and releases to the customer also do not need to be a forcing function based on the time elapsed. We should enter largely the business-as-usual mode, where we plan customer releases in a more organic way. We typically combine a body of work done over a period of time, which brings a logical benefit to the customer. One of the ways we do this is to assess if the set of work done since the last release has brought about meaningful improvements on performance, usability, stability, and so on, which makes it worth it for the customer to upgrade.

- In the 90-day dash, we had created a set of improvement work items as part of the learning and retrospectives. A lot of them would have been of relatively lower priority for the dash and hence would have been marked for later. It will be good to consider and plan for them now, ahead of scheduling a set of brand-new work. Note that, as opposed to simply starting work on them, we should reassess each item to confirm that it is still relevant and needed, or if it needs to be tweaked in any way.

Agility in execution

In the previous chapter, we talked about the importance of being A(I)-gile, meaning being Agile to incorporate changes according to ongoing advancements in AI. The execution aspect is the hardest one to keep flexible and agile. The reason for this is that, as per conventional wisdom, in the execution step, one should have a single-minded focus on the task at hand and shut off any interruptions and distractions. In the 90-day dash we had previously, we recommended keeping an eye on a newer way being available in the middle of the execution phase and trying to incorporate that change if possible. However, that dash had very little room to make changes, given we had a very tightly bound and focused 90-day outcome planned with a customer-facing production release planned at the end of it. Given that external facing commitment is not the central factor, the second phase of 90-days phase, provides reasonably more breathing room to do this better.

In this period, we recommend reviewing whether there is a newer AI model, better hardware, or software available in the market for the tasks being executed currently. The book recommends doing this approximately on a weekly basis and changing course from then on if required, to incorporate the same. Some of the things to put into practice in the execution phase to be able to achieve this successfully are as follows:

- Adopt a weekly execution rhythm. This means picking up tasks and targets for a week at a time.

- Continue the practice of 3-4 times a week team huddles that we had started in the previous 90-day period. This will give the team the opportunity to keep focused on ensuring that the week's deliverables are achieved every week.

- In parallel throughout the week, you as the manager should spend roughly 10-20% of your focus on ensuring that the version of AI your team is using is still the latest.

- Any new technology can be unstable or rough around the edges as soon as it comes out. Moreover, many times, what is promised on paper is not necessarily always seen in practice in your use case. A good example of this is when a new car is launched on the market; it typically comes with advanced features and a promise of better mileage. However, we would evaluate those for our usage pattern, road conditions, and lifestyle, by taking the car for one or more test drives before making the purchase. Similarly, if we find a newer version of AI technology or tools as compared to what we originally had in our plans, we recommend taking the following steps:

  1. Give a heads-up about this to the person working on the respective work item for which you found the potential new solutions available.

  2. We do not need to change course or abandon the task in the middle of the week itself. Rather, we can continue to bring the current week's tasks to a logical conclusion.

  3. If you or anyone in the team has time within the same week, then we should pick up the task of evaluating the newer AI model or tool within the same week. Otherwise, we should ensure to make it part of next week.

  4. Let us say that the evaluation provides good evidence that the newer version is truly an improvement, supersedes our currently used solution, and is stable and reliable enough in the production scenario. In that case, further execution should be moved to the newer version. We might need to redesign some of the components or make other similar changes to the how, and it is good to plan for that in the coming week(s).

Keeping an ear to the ground on advancements in AI

The first 90-day period was about steering the ship in the right direction as well as building confidence in AI's applicability to our scenario in a practical way. The next period of 90-days is about straightening the trajectory of the ship in the direction that we would like to continue in the steady state. In this highly evolving world of AI, this means keeping up with the advancements in AI and having a continuous channel for it. In this section, let us look at a few considerations for doing this effectively.

Letting 'B' loose

In earlier chapters, we introduced the Type B persona. These are the AI enthusiasts and oriented towards learning the latest advancements in the area of technology, especially AI. Earlier, we engaged with them and channelized their strengths and expertise in various ways in a controlled manner in various phases. In the second 90-day period, we recommend trying to let them come to their own, even further, and act as a bridge between the team and the AI world outside. Here are some of the considerations to make this happen:

- Try to keep aside a significant part of their time away instead of allocating regular work items. This will help them free up the mind space, too, for thinking beyond here and now.

- Provide them with exploratory assignments with the goal of exploring AI and other technological advancements and coming up with better ways of doing things.

- Consult with them as well as other AI experts in the team to provide Type Bs with access to newer AI tech and other external AI channels.

- Set up a frequent huddle with them and also involve a select set of technical experts in the team. The frequency can be twice a week or so, considering the overall period is just 90-days. In this huddle, they should bring ideas, new whitepapers, product documentation, and so on, published on AI in recent times, and any of their own research on advancements in AI.

Prototyping stream

To complement the learning stream on which we put our Type Bs, the book recommends adding another execution track for applying that learning and building proof of concepts and prototypes. This also fosters a culture of innovation and invention in the team right after the laser-focused 90-day execution dash. Here are some of the considerations on how to go about it:

- We should align the team members involved in this effort so that the goal here is to help the team and product stay ahead of the world and in tune with AI advancements, and set us up for the future.

- We should assure them as well that this will also help them with their own learning, and by doing this well, they will be able to make a larger impact, which will also leapfrog their career growth. As a manager, we should back this up by fulfilling this promise if they do meet these high expectations and produce good results.

- Identify and task your team's AI experts and enthusiasts, typically Type Bs, to lead these short, focused, and energetic prototyping (also known as 'hackathons') a few times in this 90-day period. Logistically, we can target setting aside 3-days every 2 or 3 weeks. This will help it to be focused as well as frequently yield meaningful results during the 90-day period.

- The prototypes should be focused on the learnings Type Bs are bringing back from the team and the happenings in the AI world mentioned in the previous section. The goal is to test the hypothesis of there being a better way to do what we are doing or solve a problem that the team had bubbled up directly or when talking to the Type Bs.

Leveraging AI leaders in and outside the company

As the world of AI is evolving very fast, it might be hard to have a reliable way to separate facts from opinions when it comes to the news and publications that come out. We can reduce this ambiguity by turning to the various AI leaders and experts we can get access to. While this will still be a mix of facts and opinions, the opinions of the AI experts are still a lot more dependable than trying to form our own, based on the data we get. The primary goal here is to validate and correct our direction and learnings from the various feedback channels and narrow down to picking the right options amongst what we are presented with.

Here are some of the considerations on how to do it:

- Let us remember that the AI is also an AI expert! At the end of every week or so, it might be a simple but effective idea to chat with some of the popular AIs, such as *ChatGPT*, *Copilot*, or *Gemini*, as well as check what is the latest in this context according to them. This can also be a fun Friday activity with the team, where as a team you can come up with questions to ask the chatbots and build a prioritized set of to-dos for the next week.

- Working with the company and organization leadership, we should identify a couple of AI leaders in the company. We should take their help for consulting and advising frequently on our thoughts and what we hear as the next big thing to adopt in the AI space.

- Either directly or indirectly via the previously mentioned AI experts of our company, we should try to get access to the opinions and views of the various experts outside the company, too. Tapping into the articles they publish, seminars or talks they conduct, and how they are shaping their own areas of ownership will be a great source of inputs to validate our own directions and bets.

Conclusion

In this chapter, we completed our AI transformation journey spanning over 6 months or so, broken down into two periods of 90-days each. We learnt how to fine-tune and polish the quick work we did in the first 90-day period. In the second 90-day period, we also opened our eyes and ears a lot more to various possible feedback channels to ensure our direction and goals are on the right track, and learnt how to get this done. We also established a few channels to validate that the outcomes and results are relevant and useful for the team and the customers. In a subtle way, some of these will help us transition first from the 90-day dash into a more planful 90-day period and later, to a more strategic and steady state going forward. The remaining two chapters of the book will cover this in detail. The next chapter takes one step forward into that by discussing a few of the important traits of living in the transformed era.

CHAPTER 9
Beyond the Tactical

Introduction

So far in the book, we assessed the AI world view, understood the composition and characteristics of our team members, found ways to transform our team and product, and concluded a six-month journey to complete the transformation.

In the previous two chapters, including this one, we will discuss a few things pertaining to strategizing for the long-term journey in the new world. We will also take a fresh look at thinking from a clean slate point of view, as opposed to managing within what we have and where we started off from.

Structure

This chapter covers the following topics:

- Communication and collaboration in AI-enhanced teams
- Decision-making with AI assistance
- Embedding AI in organizational and individual goals

Objectives

After doing the hard work to fix things, get them running, and get us to a good place, it is easy to assume that things will be self-sustaining from this point on. However, in reality, without putting in ongoing effort, the chances are that they will regress or diverge over time. This chapter will help us think about some of the steps to take to make things more future-ready. We will learn how to position AI as a strategic element in the scheme of things, as opposed to the tactical use of AI to get a set of tasks done.

We will learn about integrating AI seamlessly into the functioning of our team on various axes, such as communication, decision-making and a holistic set of goals and success measures. By the end of this chapter, we will try to fathom how to re-imagine our team, product and other things in general, in the new-age AI-first world. We will discuss a few techniques for combining various goals and outcomes, and how to integrate them well with AI to accelerate our effectiveness further as a manager and leader.

Communication and collaboration in AI-enhanced teams

For any team and organization to scale well, be effective and efficient in doing so; there are a few important aspects to get right. Communication and collaboration are two of the important ones in this regard.

Importance of communication and collaboration

To understand the importance of communication and collaboration in the context of AI-enhanced teams, let us draw a parallel with a large-scale distributed system or an assembly line in the world of manufacturing.

Each of the individual pieces in these systems is designed to do its specific job well. They are consistently improved, fine-tuned, and overhauled frequently to keep up with the demand, changing times, and evolving technology. However, at the end of the day, the overall system needs to produce the right quality and quantity of output as per the business goals. In order for that to happen, each piece of the system should pass on relevant information to the connecting piece, inform about changes or stoppages, and also work well with the other. If this does not happen, the system will not give the desired results despite the individual components functioning at their best on their own. The organization always has to live by the adage: we succeed or fail together.

In the modern age and especially in the AI-enhanced world, things are getting exponentially faster and evolving rapidly. Due to this pace of innovation, various parts of the system get out of sync faster than before and can result in the overall system regressing as opposed to progressing forward. Therefore, the leaders and members of the team should pay extra attention to the communication and collaboration aspects both within the team and with the various stakeholders.

Within the team

Let us explore the communication and collaboration within the team.

Primary objectives

For the team members, the primary objectives for communication and collaboration can be considered as follows:

- Receiving relevant knowledge required for the team member to execute their assigned tasks.

- Creating awareness of any new information that one of the team members has come to know.

- Handing off the context of ongoing work from one member to another to ensure continuity.

- Creating an information store for posterity to help reference the same in the future.

- Driving alignment on important protocols, processes and rules of engagement.

- Seeking help and asking questions if one is blocked.

- Brainstorming ideas and options before and during the execution of a task.

- Getting a review and seeking feedback on completed work.

- Passing on work items (reassigning) between multiple team members if needed.

- Break down a large piece of work item to be able to assign to more than one team member for parallel execution or logical checkpoints.

- Alignment on the contract and outside-in responsibilities of each of the pieces in the pipeline, also known as **interfaces** or **contracts** in the world of software architecture and design.

Measures of effectiveness

Some of the major indicators of effective communication and collaboration, within the team, are as follows:

- The required information and resources should be available quickly when needed.

- For the source, the effort and overhead to disseminate information should be minimal.

- The tools used should be standardized and conducive to collaboration between multiple participants.

- The source should be able to control the recipients and spread of the information based on the need. Even in the future, access to this information should not be compromised and should be controllable as well.

- It should be easy to find any relevant past communication if the same information is being asked again.

- It should be easy to find a needle in the haystack, meaning finding and extracting specific information amongst the large volume of past and ongoing communications.

- It should be possible and relatively easy to back track or connect the dots when tracing a piece of implementation to the corresponding design/contract and how that design was arrived upon.

- Sometimes, when the information is in the form of audio, it is not easily understandable due to a variety of reasons such as different accents, lack of audio clarity, low or high volume and presence of background noise. In those cases, too, the listeners should be able to have a way to extract the information with as much accuracy as possible. In case it is a recorded audio, it is not possible to interrupt the speaker and ask for clarification, and hence in those cases, this becomes even more important.

Possible AI-enhanced solutions

Here are some possible mechanisms to solve for the previously mentioned requirements and success measures for the in-team communication and collaboration:

- Use the modern communication and collaboration tools, which are intrinsically AI-enhanced and provide many of the efficiency requirements out-of-the-box. Some of the examples of collaboration tools like these could be *Microsoft Office Suite*, *Google productivity suite*, *Microsoft Teams*, *Zoom* or *Google Meet*, and so on.

- Wherever the tool has the capability for it, use an AI component as a listener to the conversation so that it can build context and respond to further prompts to summarize, paraphrase or mine the data and find specific answers.

- Increase the usage of recording and documenting most of the communications and conversations. This ensures that the information is not just stored in people's minds (also known as **tribal knowledge**) and is easy to access, process, and reuse. Refer to the following:

  o For meetings, consider always using hybrid set up by also joining the **video conferencing** (**VC**) meeting using tools like Zoom or Teams in addition to doing it in-person.

  o For meetings, consider making recordings as a standard practice. To make things easy, this has already started to come as a default option in many of the collaboration tools, such as Teams. Besides the capability to use this audio information later, recording the meetings will also help extend information even to those members who were not present at the meeting. This can help bridge the gap of time zones or different working hours of different individuals in the team, thus making collaboration effective and scalable.

o For a written form of conversation, consider using a group channel or distribution list, instead of a one-on-one message. This will enable the larger team also to be able to use this information, along with AI too, to be able to make it part of its knowledge base for easier AI-enabled and assistance.

o Build a habit of documenting, taking notes and sharing those as part of a brainstorming or other discussion such as deciding the scope of a work item. Many AI tools can now do this on your behalf if you invite them to the meeting and organize the information centrally, in a neat way for later use.

Across teams

Let us dive deeper into the communication and collaboration aspects pertaining to outside of the team, such as between two teams and other parties. For simplification, we will term these as stakeholders. Many of these aspects are similar, although slightly different from those we discussed for the scenario of communication and collaboration within the team.

Primary objectives

In our experience, the most prominent objectives of stakeholder communication and collaboration could be as follows:

- Ability to express and align on cross dependencies: their scope and timelines.

- Ability to track the progress and delivery of the dependencies.

- Ability to isolate and share relevant pieces of information where the larger data might contain sensitive stuff that is only suitable for a select set of individuals.

- Alignment on the contract and outside-in responsibilities of modules that the other team depends on, also known as **interfaces** or **contracts**.

- Ability to trace back past discussions, decisions and promises for posterity and hand-offs. Especially useful in case the person working on it changes.

- A predictable cadence of getting the information and status updated by the source of dependency.

Measures of effectiveness

Some of the major signs of effective communication and collaboration across the teams are as follows:

- The tools used should be standardized across the teams, possibly company-wide approved ones, thus minimizing the learning curve and friction.

- The mechanism should work seamlessly with the least overhead when the teams are located in different time zones or work at different times of the day.

- For each of the teams, the experience of collaborating with the other team should be pleasant and rewarding.

- The mechanism should enable information passing for positive hand-offs between the teams, similar to passing of the baton in a relay race.

- In case of change of hands or responsibilities inside a team, the incoming person should have a quick and easy way to get the gist of the status of the engagement and progress, and what is needed from them. This enables the new team member to get going quickly without any noticeable impact on the activity that otherwise might have happened due to a change of personnel.

Advantage with AI-enhanced solutions

Most of the popular collaboration tools are rapidly evolving to incorporate AI advancements to fully leverage the capabilities of AI. Some of the advantages they are trying to bring are as follows:

- AI can summarize a long conversation or engagement at any point of time when needed.

  ○ This is especially useful when there is a change of hands for the new person to quickly learn what their team is expected to do from now on.

o When a new stakeholder joins the collaboration, AI can detect that and provide a summary automatically to them to get them started.

o For the important engagements, AI can help prepare a crisp update which can be shared with leadership to be able to provide them with a top-level, accurate gist on an ongoing basis without much human effort.

o AI provides the capability to personalize the verbosity, composition, and tone of the summary by any participant or any team based on their preference or depending on the intended receiver of it.

- By integrating with AI-enhanced software, such as AI-agents, the tool can provide additional efficiency and accuracy benefits, such as the following:

  o When multiple teams are involved, the AI agent can determine which team should be notified or assigned the next step. It can do this based on some pre-defined rules, as well as infer from the context of the conversation or work item. This will save a lot of time and human effort and speed up the throughput of the entire engagement.

  o If this were being done by humans, they are not mandated to have a feedback loop. Thus, it is left to them whether they learn from the mistakes and improve or continue doing things in the same way. Moreover, in a team, there are usually new people joining and existing people leaving, and in those cases, the context and training the human received were lost in the transition. On the other hand, AI can continuously learn from any mistakes it makes and keep yielding better accuracy and speed.

  o It is well-established that if humans are doing similar kinds of tasks repeatedly, their effectiveness decreases with time, and mistakes can creep into the output. With some additional features like time-based or event-based scheduling of tasks, AI agent can circumvent the errors or delays that can be caused by human-based execution.

- AI can reduce the need for the person to reach out to others if he or she is blocked on some information or direction. Some of the ways it can help are as follows:

o AI can be trained on the existing and new incoming information base, to have conversational capability to find answers quickly. An example of this could be in the healthcare sector, where if a patient's file is advanced to another specialist or another department, they can get a fairly accurate summary of what treatment or diagnosis was done so far and then resume from there.

o If presented with a situation, humans can find if a similar situation has happened earlier and what was done in that case. However, they cannot typically easily extract patterns and approximate matches amongst a large volume of past occurrences. On the other hand, advanced AI, such as **generative AI (GenAI)** or AI agents can easily find patterns and close matches and aid in applying the same solution easily to the new situation. An example of this could be in a customer support organization where a large number of customer issues might be on similar lines or can be categorized into a finite number of buckets, but are not exactly the same.

Decision-making with AI assistance

Making many decisions day in and day out is integral to strategic thinking and being for a manager and for their team. Some of the dimensions for these decisions could be as follows:

- Product roadmap
- Strategic direction of the team
- Individual roles and responsibilities
- Prioritization of work
- Prioritization of investments

Traditionally, decision-making is a nuanced activity and involves a combination of using available data, trends, intuition, taking into account the sensibilities and preferences of the people involved in a decision and so on. In this section, we will evaluate how we can make such critical decisions with the help of AI.

Putting multi-dimensional data together

Most decision-makers, as well as those who are in charge of recommending insights and actions, often have access to a large amount of useful data to help them. However, accurate processing and analysis of multiple dimensions and large volumes of data is often limited by the experience, knowledge and bandwidth of the human looking at it. AI models and tools have reached the maturity and scale where they can easily make sense of huge volumes of data, containing multiple dimensions and often lacking any structure. They can provide a summary, offer insights or even recommendations based on the data when asked specific questions. This can elevate the effectiveness of the decision-maker manyfold, and also ensure taking out human errors in maximizing the power of data in decision-making.

Testing the waters

One of the challenges when it comes to high-stakes decisions is that it is hard to know how things will turn out after implementing that decision. It does not matter how thorough we have been; considering all signals and inputs, and potential outcomes of it, it is not possible to really know the outcome until things are implemented and run. One of the significant sources of this unpredictability is the different people who might be involved, wherein it is not possible to know whether they will react in favor or against the change. An example of this could be rolling out a new feature that we think will benefit the customers, but we realize after checking with early adopters that the change was too drastic and they do not like it.

Would it not be great if we could have somehow played it out and known this in advance? It could have saved us and the team all the effort of making things customer-ready, getting this in the customer's hands, pursuing them to try it and give us feedback, and then having to take many steps back, and in the end, go back to the drawing board.

Earlier in the book, we saw that one of the possible use cases of AI is to present itself as a simulated user or a group of users. This user can be customized to take on a persona of our choice. Once provided with the context, it can be our simulated version of a real person;

in this case, a set of customers. We can run these new changes or product features with this customer and get the feedback fairly early in the cycle. This can help us modify or replan our decisions and increase the chances of success when we eventually implement them.

Objectivity in decision-making

Despite our best intentions, utilizing best practices and being data-driven, the final decision does have a flavor of who made it. It is inherently influenced by biases, prejudices, specific experiences, and, many times, agendas. Many times, as they say, it is a hard problem to separate facts from opinions, experience from fears, data from the lens it is being viewed, and so on. The other angle is if the people in-charge change, the decisions made by the previous personnel might not be aligned to the sensibilities of the new personnel. In those cases, the entire organization might get into a state of cascading impact of this misalignment and back and forth. This could be prevented or minimized if the decision-making is as objective as possible.

Modern AI is still evolving in a few aspects. However, it can help us bring utmost objectivity into making those high-stakes decisions. It has the capability of analyzing, reasoning, thinking and coming up with recommendations, directions, or a complete pros-cons analysis of various options to make the decisions highly objective.

Embedding AI in organizational and individual goals

One of the important guiding factors for the team and the organization is the goals they are entrusted with. Therefore, to truly AI-fy the team and organization for the long-term, it is essential that the AI is embedded seamlessly in those goals. Let us look at how we can go about making that happen.

AI-fied organizational goals

As AI evolves, it has been getting increasingly more adept at taking up complex and multifaceted tasks, and its use in each of the goals can be a great differentiator. Let us look at some considerations on how to integrate AI into various organizational goals.

Goals pertaining to the product and business

The organization usually has goals around product and business, such as revenue, adaptation, and engagement targets. There are non-functional goals as well, such as availability, reliability, cost, and performance, which are promised to the customers to ensure a fair value for money and predictable quality of service for the customers.

AI can be an important cog in the wheel here in a few ways, such as:

- Goals around the proportion of AI used for measuring and tracking these.

- Goals around the adoption of the most prominent AI tools in the domain.

- Forecasting and recommendations using AI.

- Reporting and insights on numbers.

Goals around cost and budget

The next important category of goals an organization typically has is around planning and managing costs and budgets for various categories of expenses. The target is to rationalize spending on different things such as infrastructure, technology, operational expenditure, sales, marketing, workforce, travel and entertainment, learning, conferences, and so on. AI can be part of this in a few different ways:

- Incentivizing teams to evaluate and negotiate more cost-effective AI-based tools.

- Incentivizing teams to be more innovative and use AI-based opportunities such as better prompt engineering, AI-agents, and so on, to be able to do 'more with less'.

- Goals around incorporating AI and doing AI-based innovations in the customer support and engagement aspects for more cost-effective ways for the customer feedback channel.

- Using AI in day-to-day tasks for finding the best cost for things such as travel, logistics, and so on.

- For software and infrastructure costs as well, AI can help with things such as building an optimized architecture that needs the least footprint. This can include taking AI's help to analyze the usage patterns for demand forecasting and suggesting dynamic scale up and down, based on things like time of the day, peak or off-season, and customer distribution in specific geographies.

Goals around velocity and output of the team

While the previous two categories are more of outside-in or around 'what' the business needs to do, there are also goals that the leaders of the organization have around 'how' the business is executed. One of the obvious goals is around the capability and speed of delivery and innovation of the various teams in the organization. They are expected to have similar or better numbers than organizations with similar size, market cap, or customer base.

In the AI era, one of the automatic ways to keep parity is to drive goals in their teams around the adoption and engagement of the relevant AI tools and technology. As well as incentivize and reward those who do it first or come up with new and innovative ways to use AI for doing the same work faster, or more work in less time or resources.

AI-fied individual goals

As previously discussed, for a manager, making the goals personalized to each individual and linking them to the learning and growth of each team member is a great objective to strive for. In doing so, one should first understand and align the needs and wants of individuals in the team. We should aim to learn things like the following:

- Their career objectives at the moment are: say, new in role, seasoned, and looking for growth, or need to try something new.

- What are the skills and strengths each of them needs to exercise and improve?

- What are the areas of improvement that were identified for each of them?

With these questions and objectives in mind, let us look at how we can go about it and how AI can be an integral part of it.

Building depth and knowledge

For those team members who are new to their role or are learning new skills or building context in the current product and technology, AI can be a great ally and guide in their journey. For example, AI can fast-track its effort to learn the gist of the organization of code or details of the current design of the product. Many of the **integrated development environments** (IDE) and developer tools are coming up with AI-integrated out-of-the-box, where they can be trained on the large code base of the product and then can help answer many questions. These could be on the lines of the following:

- What are the major big pieces of building blocks in this code base?
- What is this function or class designed for?
- What are the interfaces this module exports?

Similar to this, AI-integrated software design and **user experience** (**UX**) tools can help one quickly get the summary and narrative of the underlying document and build the basic context to be able to go deeper and work on advancing or enhancing the existing product. This means they can rapidly become an advanced developer without having to spend many years building context or having to be part of the making process to understand the nuances of different pieces.

The measurable goal to demonstrate their increased knowledge could be expressed in terms of increased complexity and quality of work they can deliver while sustaining or increasing their throughput and velocity.

Improving productivity

For those team members whose productivity is a concern or an area of improvement, adding increased reliance on AI as a goal could be an obvious step. As a manager, you can make the 'what' of improving productivity as well as the 'how' of visibly demonstrating their increase in usage of AI, as a meaningful way of achieving this.

It is always recommended to define the goals in a measurable way. In this case, we should use the benchmark of productivity needed from individuals in the team as the premise and come up with the metric accordingly as the 'what' goal. Adoption of AI to achieve this 'what' can also be defined as a 'how' goal too. We can think in terms of % of work done using AI or % of total tasks completed using AI on a weekly or monthly basis.

We could also encourage them to periodically share the creative and new ways they learnt in their work to improve productivity and finesse with others in the team. They can also be coined as the drivers for productivity and AI-adoption for your team or larger organization as well, and that can be an even more impactful goal. This will additionally help you as the manager to drive productivity and beneficial AI-adoption in your team, too.

Advancing key skills

While we have used AI to help get many of the tasks completed faster or better, we can also use it for learning and advancing key skills required for the job. Apart from those who are looking to learn new skills in general, this could be even more useful for the team members who have done well in their current role and are looking to advance to take on a bigger role or to get into a different role. Here are a few examples of this:

- An engineer looking to get into a role of an architect.
- An individual contributor looking to become a lead or a manager.
- A technical person, such as a software engineer, wanting to get into a product management role.

While a seasoned performer in a former role brings in a track record and confidence that they will succeed in the new role, it is essential to realize that each role has a different set of key skills that are required. Success in one role is not necessarily a guarantee for success in a different role, and one should strive to bridge the skill gap before or during early days of taking on a new role. AI, or even one of the popular conversational AIs, such as *ChatGPT*, *Copilot* or *Gemini*, among others, can help the person go about their learning and skill building in an effective and efficient manner. Here are some sample questions that the team member can ask these bots about:

- What are the key skills I should learn for my new role as a software architect?

- I have been a C++ developer for 10 years and now I am entering the world of python. What are the nuances I should learn to quickly become an expert at python while leveraging my existing knowledge and experience?

- I want to advance my skills of storytelling as I am taking on a strategic product management role. What are the trainings or courses I should take?

- I have been a good engineer for 12 years and I am being trusted with a managerial role. What is a good first set of training and knowledge bases that I can utilize to transition into a role as a manager in the next three-months?

Conclusion

In this chapter, we learned a few dimensions of seamlessly integrating AI for strategic existence of the team, product and organization. We learnt how to transform communication, collaboration and goals to make them AI-fied and also utilize AI for the transformation itself into the new way of being. This chapter should give actionable steps to the manager and the organization to enter and live in the AI era in the near future.

This leads us into the last chapter of the book, which will attempt to plant seeds for the future in one's journey as a manager and leader. Our focus so far has been on both short-term and strategic transformation of the existing product and team, owing to the AI era. However, the concluding chapter will set the stage for the reader as a manager to think afresh about leadership and how to go about becoming a revolutionary leader in times of change.

Join our Discord space

Join our Discord workspace for latest updates, offers, tech happenings around the world, new releases, and sessions with the authors:

https://discord.bpbonline.com

Chapter 10
Planting Seeds for the Future

Introduction

We think that the **artificial intelligence (AI)** age is the start of a new wave of transformation and innovation in the world of technology. We believe that it is imperative to think and live differently in order to survive as well as thrive. While the future is not known and the landscape is evolving at a fast pace, there are a few ways we can approach things going forward to maximize the chances of success. In this concluding chapter, the book attempts to come up with some food for thought about planting those seeds for the future in you as a leader and those leaders of the future you might be grooming. We will discuss a few strategies for transforming oneself and the team to become more dynamic and more conducive to similar waves of change that might be coming in the future, and not just AI.

Structure

This chapter covers the following topics:

- Designing teams for the AI age

- Aspiring to innovation as the new AI
- Open up to the disruptive way of working

Objectives

In this chapter, we will learn how a manager can orient themselves and their teams for a new way of thinking and operating. We will look at the skills and traits we believe will help build oneself and the team of future. The chapter will also discuss how to go about the journey of transformation for future based on your specific evolution phase. By the end of this chapter and also the book, the reader should be able to prepare themselves for leading or building a team for success in the times to come, including and beyond the current AI wave.

Designing teams for the AI age

In the majority of the book, our approach for AI-fication was to work with the existing team and try to take things forward in the best way possible. This approach assumes that we have more or less the right ingredients in the team, and the changes we need to bring are not too drastic to need a major overhaul. However, that is not always the case. There are times when the gaps are much larger, and we have to rebuild or build teams from scratch to succeed in the AI-enabled world. Another scenario could be when you, as the leader, take on a new charter and are given the opportunity to build things your own way from the start. Even otherwise, once the transformation is complete, for sustained success, we should look at the holistic picture and ensure our team is indeed designed for the AI age going forward.

Regardless of the use case, thinking afresh and top-down is a great skill for a manager to have to succeed in the dynamic world. Let us look at a few considerations on how we can approach those cases. Before we begin, it must be noted that we are not suggesting completely throwing away the existing team and hiring new personnel altogether in order to succeed. Rather, we will have a more practical and planful approach. We will discuss this further in this section.

Skillset for success

AI as a technology is evolving, and everyone definitely needs to build technical expertise around AI. In this subsection, we will talk about some of the other traits and ways of thinking we should strive for in order to build a team for the AI age and beyond.

Being a problem solver

First and foremost, the most important trait we would need in team members is the mindset of solving problems and finding the best solution for them. Once we start to find the best possible solution for the given problem, chances are that AI or another latest innovative technology out there will generally be a winner for most problems we are looking to solve. This way, one will automatically become more and more in tune with the evolving times.

Here are some of the characteristics to look for or inculcate in someone for this trait:

- They look forward to solving problems as opposed to running away or avoiding them.
- They are resourceful and always feel like they have a plan.
- They get energy by seeing problems solved away, needles moving, and things advancing further.
- They take up a problem and do what is necessary to figure out and try to solve it.

Excited about possibilities and change

There is a saying that *small minds talk about people; average minds talk about events, and great minds talk about ideas.* Ideas mean possibilities. The AI age and beyond is all about opening our minds to possibilities and not being scared of change.

Here are some of the key characteristics of this trait:

- They are capable of thinking beyond what others can see, that is, strategic thinkers.
- They thrive and get energized by ambiguity as opposed to looking for a clear line of sight to achieve goals.

- They get bored easily and thus always want to change, optimize, improve, innovate. Yes, you read that right, boredom can indeed be a positive trait!

Learning and growth mindset

In our experience, this trait is one of the hardest to find, especially in seasoned professionals. The reason is that as one gains experience, they acquire a lot of knowledge and successes under their belt. Hence, it is imperative that they believe what they know and how they do things is the right way. It takes a lot to always look at everything from a fresh mindset and not presume it fits what they already know. In the case of AI age and beyond, one should not be attached to and boxed into existing tools, technology and knowledge. AI itself is evolving extremely rapidly, and the pace of innovation is expected to remain hyper, at least for a few more years to come until it reaches its full potential. There might be a pause or slowdown after that, but that might last only until the next new innovation after AI comes to the fore.

Here are some key characteristics of this trait:

- These folks are always the first to break the news about new happenings.

- They are generally curious and ask many questions.

- They might have a tendency to diverge from reaching the solution to the problem at hand and need to be brought back.

- They are open-minded and less judgmental about most topics.

Positive but pragmatic

Another fairly close term for this trait is cautiously optimistic. AI age can be quite nerve-wrecking for many professionals, given that AI is perceived as being capable of replacing humans in most cases. Thus, many of us might be feeling an identity crisis of sorts. In this adage, those who remain positive are rare but more likely to succeed, given that they will continue to put their best foot forward. Additionally, their optimism would rub off on many others too, increasing the chances of success for the team overall as well. Although plain positivity might result in empty happiness and a sense of denial. Hence, a slight mix of practicality and pragmatism is the perfect composition to ground this and make one effective in this age.

Here are a few key characteristics we can strive for:

- They are inherently not insecure individuals and are quietly confident in their abilities.

- They usually practice trust, but verify meaning they are cautious but not paranoid.

- They are open to taking calculated and bold risks but take their time to think and plan to ensure success.

Agile thinker

Another term for this is thinking on one's feet. Any mature industry and any role in that is a lot about applying the knowledge, thinking through, and going with a tried and tested approach to ensure success. Being well-prepared is an essential trait for keeping everyone's nerves calm and keeping everyone confident in the plan to succeed. The AI age needs us to reverse this in some sense. In the AI age and beyond, we should have a mindset to be open to taking in late changes to our plan and not keep going despite new information coming to light. This is crucial to fail fast and not continue to spend energy in the wrong or stale direction.

Here are some of the key characteristics pertaining to this trait:

- They are good improvisers as opposed to overly rehearsing to the last possible detail.

- They are good listeners and not defensive when their approach is questioned in a constructive way.

- They are confident about their approach but they typically socialize it with a few others and discuss rather than being on their own.

Team composition to strive for

Next, just like a perfect recipe for a perfect cuisine, let us look at the composition and proportion of each of the ingredients we should strive to have in the team. While we talked about the traits we should strive for to have in each team member, the way those traits manifest and their proportions are different in each individual. Hence, we can picture it in terms of different personas. Let us look at what that means and what should be our team's composition of those individual ingredients.

Thinkers and planners

We need those who focus on thinking, planning, and hence setting up direction and path for the team to march on. Even in the rampant age of AI, we need to be planful and thoughtful as a team. Hence, this persona is needed in the team for success and staying ahead. There is no magic formula, but we believe that at least around a third of the team members should have this as the manifestation of their traits. Generally, having the seniormost members in the team exhibiting this persona will be an ideal foundation for the rest of the team.

Triers and fail-fasters

The AI age and future needs us to be both trying new avenues as well as having the wisdom to pause and turn back at the right time if the direction does not seem to be yielding the right results. On average, every team member should strive to build this skill. But we think that around 20-30% of team members should be operating as this persona. If the majority of them are those with mid-range experience, it will be perfect icing on the cake. This is because this skill requires a bit of prior learning of what works and what does not work to be able to make the right trade-off of when to keep going and when to stop.

Heads-down executors

At the end of the day, any team's success or lack thereof hinges on what it finally delivers. It is hard to measure the success of ideas or experiments. It is imperative to have a result-oriented mindset in the team so the team self-regulates itself on the grounds of so what, meaning what was the measurable outcome of our efforts. This helps the team make the best out of their efforts and continue to solve problems for customers as opposed to marinating in ideas and new technology. We believe everyone in the team should be capable of wearing this hat when needed. But in terms of exhibiting this persona, we think that 40-50% of the team should be operating in this mode so that we make progress and deliver results in a timely manner. Ideally, the majority of these could be those who are early in their careers and still gaining experience. They will generally be at their best when given clear instructions and deliverables without being constantly interrupted due to changes or re-scoping of the plans.

Going about building or rebuilding the team

Let us now look at how to navigate the journey of where the team currently is and where we want it to reach. We will consider both scenarios, whether we are building a brand-new team or starting with an existing team with gaps to fill, to arrive at the ideal design.

Formulating the first set of goals

When embarking on this journey, it is imperative to first define the set of goals of the new team or the team in the new avatar. These goals should ideally be a mix of business goals, team evolution goals and sometimes 'how' goals too. Here are a few suggestions on how to decide these goals:

- **Business goal**: Small features or improvements in the backlog that are important but not urgent. Features where 'what' and to some extent 'how' is fairly clear and thus contain minimal ambiguity.

- **Evolution goal**: You and the team have gone through relevant knowledge transfer to be able to ask the right questions and have a point of view. The number of meeting hours is reducing, especially for the individual contributors in the team.

- **How goal**: The team is able to execute independently or with minimal expert help. The execution is completed within or very close to the timeline as per the initial estimation of the majority of tasks.

Nucleus of the team

The first thing to focus on is the nucleus of the team. The easy way to think about the nucleus is those who can be the future leaders in the team from both a mindset perspective as well as from their domain and technical expertise perspective. Let us envision the team as a set of concentric circles and the manager at the center of it. In that model, these team members can be considered as the innermost circle (thus the nucleus analogy), closely aligned with the center. They are expected to play the role of the agents for helping fan out and scale the leader's vision and direction in the rest of the team.

Let us consider a few scenarios:

- If we are building a new team, we should focus on hiring and consolidating the nucleus first. We should give the journey the time for them to settle, come up to speed and get to a steady state, that is, operating at their fullest potential.

- If we have an existing team, this would mean identifying those who can be considered as the nucleus of the team and focusing on any preparations or tweaks to get them to operate as such.

- If we have an existing team, but the composition of the team does not seem to naturally have a nucleus, we should plan how to fill the gap. Depending upon the specific situation, we should combine hiring a few new team members and grooming a few of the existing team members. Keeping a few of the existing team members into the nucleus helps to avoid throwing the team in a full pause or reset as the new members need time to completely come into their own. Similarly, hiring a few new members adds to the missing skillset of the team, whereas grooming those in the team would be extremely time-consuming and would halt progress for some time.

Few key master executors

Once we have a strategy identified for forming a nucleus of the team and have started working on building it, we should start getting in a few members who are known for their solid execution skills. This will help us achieve quick wins (we will see this again in the next subsection) even in the building or re-building phase and also will help us set the foundation of the ways of working in the team. This will include the key processes, tools, best practices and the expected velocity which we will use as the reference point for the rest of the team going forward.

Similar to the various scenarios in the context of the nucleus, here are a few for this set as well:

- If we are building a new team, it is wise to not go too fast or too big on hiring the execution focused members right away. This is because, in the beginning there is likely to be a lack of clarity and dearth of people to create the plan for the execution focused individuals to work on. This might result in wasted cycles and a lack of motivation amongst the team.

- If we have an existing team, this would mean identifying those who have a track record of solid estimation, delivery and ability to execute on a given plan without getting sidetracked. However, we should time this depending on whether or not the nucleus is in place.

- If we have an existing team, but the composition of the team does not seem to have pure, solid executors, we need to fill the gap by hiring a few new team members who are hungry to contribute. The rest of the existing team members are best utilized either as a part of the nucleus or for later. This is because typically they would have a good context and knowledge of the area and it would not be fair and effective to have them to just execute on pre-decided tasks and thus not utilize their full capability. If things are going to take longer before their turn comes, we can also have a conversation with them to decide if their skills will be better utilized elsewhere and help find a rightful home for them.

Rest of the team-building journey

Once we have the initial set of goals and key members in place, we should go about the construction and delivery journey. Let us look at the set of considerations and steps we can take from this point onwards:

1. As we briefly mentioned in the previous subsection, we should identify a set of quick wins to target, especially when most of the team members are newly hired, either the

nucleus or the executors. We should get the team to focus on achieving those first.

2.   We should assess the timeframe for achieving the state of having the new AI age team in place. We should find out what the leadership expects, what generally is the industry standard and the extent of the gap we are trying to fill (e.g., we mostly have all the team we need or a large part of the new team still needs to be hired or groomed). It could be a number of weeks, months, semesters, etc. This will help decide the speed at which we need to run and also the frequency of checkpoints and other things.

3.   After knowing the overall timeframe, we should divide that into a set of evolution milestones and set some goals for each milestone. It will help us have a method to madness at all times during the journey. It will also give us a framework and feedback loop to know if we are on the right track to learn and adjust accordingly. We should form the intermittent milestones and success measures in terms of the first set of goals we introduced earlier in this chapter.

Aspiring to innovation as the new AI

The AI wave is an example of the larger concept of innovation in the industry and the world at large. The leaders and the teams that not just survive but thrive over a large period of time are those who are always looking for opportunities to innovate. With them, innovation is not an afterthought or additive but a way of working and living. Any leader who thinks and models the strategic way of working should strive to aspire to continuous innovation.

Essence of innovation

Innovation is a well-known term in the language but is often misunderstood as something fancy or additive. The popular belief about innovation is that it is something really big, needs extensive research or resources and means throwing away everything we have. However, as per the well-renowned *Cambridge Dictionary*, the word 'innovation' denotes 'a new idea or method'. If we zoom in on the word 'new', one of the primary meanings, as per the same dictionary, is 'different from one that existed earlier'. Putting these together, the act of innovation is simply about having an idea or method that did not exist earlier.

Aspiring for innovation implies that we should not be settled in a comfort zone or routine. Rather, think of that as a sign of stagnation and instead look for better ways of doing anything we see around us. There are several examples around this, both in real life and in the world of science. For example, stagnant water is not considered pristine, and over a period of time, it becomes rotten and spoiled, which is not useful for any good purpose. In the world of science and technology, everything from the smallest of things, such as atoms, to the largest of things, such as planets and stars, is always moving as well as evolving. Time does not stop for anyone, and whether we like it or not, everything, including us, moves to the next second with every passing second.

Types of innovations

The best innovations are those that evolve an existing solution further, also popularly known as the **better mouse trap**. The reason is that it is easy to test for functionality and effectiveness when there is an existing benchmark to compare it with. Also, the users know that the problem indeed exists, thus the adaptation of the solution and chances of your success will be higher. Lastly, we as humans tend to get bored very quickly, more so in the age of OTT apps and social media, where our attention spans are getting shorter by the day. Always looking for something to change the monotony can help make things more interesting for us as well as everyone around us.

It is important to note that the proportion of ideas and innovations that actually succeed and go any further is relatively small. That makes it even more important to come up with many more of these ideas and proposals so that a few can go through and take us to any meaningful success. We often hear that life is not perfect. As a corollary, there must be problems and inefficiencies in abundance. Hence, it should be possible, once you start thinking that way, to find possible problems and potential new solutions for them everywhere we look.

Reasons to aspire to continuous innovation

History has shown us that every major wave of innovation brings about a change of guard in the industry. Many well-established industry-leading organizations are being replaced at the top by new and innovative ones. However, there are many renowned organizations that continue to keep their brand value and position in the market as they are either ahead of the curve or are flexible and evolve by embracing the new wave. Several examples in the technology industry, such as *Nokia* and *Blackberry* when the smartphone revolution swept the world or *IBM* when the PC wave came or *Intel* when the GPU wave swept up, are testimony of the former. We have another famous example of *Blockbuster* and *Netflix* change of guard when the internet speeds and streaming technology crossed the threshold of making online streaming more affordable and efficient as compared to mailing DVDs.

On the other side of the spectrum, stalwarts like *Google*, *Microsoft*, *Amazon*, and *Samsung* continue to stand tall and grow from strength to strength, withstanding many decades of world-changing technology innovations coming to the fore. It must be noted that there would be other factors also contributing to the success or lack of it, but it is undeniable that a major factor continues to be the changing landscape of technology and customer expectations, and the organization's ability to adapt to them.

Inspiring innovation

Let us now discuss how a manager can inspire a culture of innovation in their team. Just like for other changes, we believe that managers should lead by example in this case as well. As they say, 'show, not tell'. In their day-to-day tasks and actions, a manager should try to demonstrate how they are being innovative. It can be embracing new ways of doing things, evangelizing new developments happening around us, or sharing their own experience and best practices for the team to learn from. Another simple but powerful outcome could be that the more we put technology to do our work, the more time is saved and the more we appear as more cheerful and friendly. The manager's mood and mannerisms rub off on the team very quickly in a subconscious way, even without trying, and hence if they see innovative ways working for you, they will also start to follow suit.

Well begun is half done. Leading by example moves the needle of inspiring innovation, but we need to do a few more things to utilize this momentum. Here are a few suggestions:

- To use the momentum of *show, do tell* as well. Essentially, do not shy away from making suggestions when you see gaps or opportunities to do things in a better way. This ensures that the team is receiving clear communication and direction to renew the mission and also revalidate that innovation is still relevant and is at the top of their leaders' minds.

- To complement an innovative mindset, using a positive tone, mannerisms, and language when talking about gaps and innovative ideas is also something which the manager should consciously exercise and, over a period of time, make it part of them. What we say is important, but how we say it is even more important and can enhance the impact and intensity of our message, and this scenario is no exception.

- Time to time, the managers themselves also taking up the tasks of doing some of the proof of concepts and prototyping will be a good idea. This also shows the team how to do it, but also builds a lot of confidence and respect for the manager as being one amongst them.

Open up to the disruptive way of working

Let us talk about a different aspect when it comes to evolution and innovation. We are taught that the way to succeed in the technology domain is to spend time, go deep, build expertise and that is the way one can make a major impact. To grow into a role of senior engineer or architect, one needs to master the specific technology, programming language, etc. Let us look deeper.

Stability is important

The argument of sticking to the same technology in order to grow is also supported by the fact that technology, such as programming language, operating system, utility software like word processing systems, spreadsheet technologies, presentation software, and so on, has remained relevant and popular for a really long time. The most relevant and most widely used programming languages of today, C, C++, Java, Golang, etc., have been around for multiple decades. Even the most popular modern language, Python, was invented more than 30 years ago. The most popular consumer operating systems: Windows, Mac, and others, are multiple decades old. While they keep adding features and new innovations, inherently their success relies on the users being accustomed and familiar with how to do their tasks using these operating systems. Similar examples can be found in any industry, such as manufacturing, which traditionally used to move at a much slower rate. In fact, the world of technology is considered one of the fastest-moving, but there, too, as we saw just now, things have been relatively stable for many decades.

Reasons we do not think differently

While this concept of impact and time is still relevant and important, many of us interpret this to be the case of the status quo of technology being a key factor for learning and growth in this context. Any new innovation that breaks on the scene, we are accustomed to letting it settle and run the test of time before it can be widely acknowledged as important and worth adopting. Hence, for most professionals working in a vast majority of industries, disruption in the technology world is considered a distraction and the opposite of stability and growth.

As seasoned managers, we deem our job to provide clarity, predictability, and minimize disruptions to what the team members are expected to do. We spend a large amount of time and effort planning, and then we expect those plans to be implemented by the team. We try to protect the team from any kind of external noise that can derail the plans and make the execution inefficient. Due to this, our tendency becomes one of avoiding or squashing any drastic inputs coming from outside or within the team, or to look at it from a skeptical lens.

To be able to shield the execution from uncertain, half-baked or non-data-driven distractions is a great trait for a manager and an important sign of them becoming really good at efficient execution. Many of the early managers struggle to keep their plans on track because there is so much new input that keeps coming in the middle of the execution period from customers, leadership, or new developments coming across from the news. Hence, to a large extent, pushing back on a disruptive way of doing things can be considered a goal to aspire to and a sign of growth for a manager.

Reasons a change is needed

The last couple of years, which have been a breakthrough period for AI and exponential innovation, have challenged many practices traditionally considered the right way of doing things. The concepts of stability and disruption are also among those. The speed of useful change and relevant innovation is multiplying and is something that we cannot afford to ignore or push back anymore. The trend so far, in the last 5 to 10 years, was that new concepts used to pop up every few weeks, threatening to change the traditional ways, get popular quickly, and then disappear because when they were really battle-tested, they could not survive.

The trend now has become, and will likely remain for a long time, that there is an innovation that comes in every one to 2 weeks, dwarfs the previous solution, gets really popular, and the world scrambles to adapt it and leave the old one behind. The providers of the older version quickly deprioritize them because there is not much return on investment anymore, as those are no longer in demand by the customers. Examples of these are newer AI models, including the advent of new paradigms like *DeepSeek*. It is not necessary that every innovation is successful, but how the innovations are looked at and treated by the world has evolved rapidly. Hence, if we ignore such disruptions and stick to our original plans, chances are that we will spend time building something which will not be useful anymore, leading to a larger number of wasted cycles than if we had stopped mid-way and changed direction.

What disruptive way looks like

Let us clarify that our argument is not that we should derail our execution and plan for every disruption and interruption. We still need to have an execution plan and do everything to make it successful, including keeping the blinders on and executing. Let us look at a few aspects where we are recommending doing things differently.

Way of thinking

Instead of being apprehensive about new proposals, an innovative and future-looking manager should welcome them. One should assess them in a bit more detail, spend some discussion and brainstorming time to completely understand and to be able to make a more informed decision about adapting or discarding the idea. The more radical the idea is, the more attention it deserves, is the way to embrace a disruptive way of thinking. Getting genuinely excited each time you hear someone suggesting that there is something new in the town, or there is a better way of doing something, or that they are finding what they are doing as uninteresting, is a great behavior to develop. This will help one seek possibilities of efficiency, productivity and a better way of doing things on an ongoing basis. Not to mention, the team, leadership and stakeholders will also look forward to collaborating with you more as they would like to rally behind a progressive and welcoming leader. Over a period of time, you will be able to calibrate yourself and build skills to differentiate substance from fluff without wasting a lot of time.

Planning and execution

Planning can be challenging when you know that there are factors that will make the plan irrelevant very quickly. In reality, this is not an all-or-nothing scenario. The intent should always be to plan diligently and do all it takes to ensure the plan is respected during the execution and taken to completion. Hence, while we need to facilitate changes, there needs to be a system in place to ensure that changes do not keep seeping in all the time and make the plan meaningless. A few ways to ensure this are as follows:

- Decide the degree of disruption of the plan you want to target, call it the disruption budget. This means that we are prepared to have the plan change by that much %. To give a guideline around this, if dealing with mostly known things, this can be 5-10% whereas when your area is fast changing, it can be as high as 40-50%.

- The work items picked in the unit of execution should have clear priority as always, but also, the amount of must-do's we pick should be in proportion to the possible disruption %. For example, if we decided the disruption budget to be 30%, then only up to 70% of the work items should be the ones that we cannot afford to slip or postpone.

- While assigning work to individuals, try to have a target of earmarking those who we should try to protect from changes during execution and have an idea of which all team members should be ready in case a change comes. Essentially, the disruption % should not be distributed to the entire team. This will ensure that the effects of any disruption that might come in during execution are contained and do not result in stop-start and thus wasted cycles for everyone in the team unnecessarily.

- Decide the frequency of opening the doors for changes in the execution cycle. For example, if your execution rhythm is 2 weeks, consider having a window once a week for bringing in changes else everything continues as originally planned.

- Keep some bandwidth for the discussions and mini-prototypes to consider the newer ideas and disruptions.

- When changing direction or picking up a new idea to execute mid-way, consider dropping or postponing the work items that were not the most critical ones, as previously decided.

Messaging to the team

While the manager knows what they are trying to do and has clarity, it is not necessary that the team understands the rationale of every decision we are making. As well as we want to keep them in their most productive state as much as possible and thus do not want to have the need for discussions and meetings every time we make a change to the execution direction. Hence, we should work on communicating the mission and methodology to them upfront and clearly. We might also need to repeat this a few times, but we should start by proactively communicating this as opposed to waiting for questions or problems to surface. Here are a few considerations in this context:

- Present the why of this methodology to your team members in the planning phase, including setting goals and disruption % for the next execution cycle.

- Clarify that the plan is always to be considered the source of truth unless we explicitly discuss and make a change.

- Communicate the label of each work item as must vs open to dropping in case of change. This can also be termed as **prioritization**.

- Have a room for dialogue and addressing questions and concerns.

Measure of individual success

Lastly, it can be very challenging for a manager to assess the performance and impact of their team members when things are changing, work can be stopped mid-way, direction can change more often than usual, and so on. We recommend the manager to take into consideration how they did their job during each step of the way and not just whether their work finally made it to the customer or not. Let us take a few examples and considerations.

- A feature went through the design phase, initial phase of coding, but then was deprioritized because its change was brought in due to a superior technology coming to light. In this case, the team member would have ended up spending most of their time on something that did not have a customer impact. We should have a closer look at how their performance was during whatever they worked on, namely the design of the feature. Consider looking deeply at whether they went about it methodically, considered different options, had a systematic and data-driven way to pick the final option and got the design reviewed and approved by the right stakeholders.

- As a result of a change, we picked up a simpler way of building a feature. This work was given to a team member who completed it fairly quickly and released it to production. While assessing this team member's performance, we should not just look at the final outcome. Instead, we should also consider whether they still executed things correctly and diligently, instead of taking any shortcuts to get things completed quickly because it was easy to begin with.

- A way to account for the team members to bring up ideas and driving decision-making for them by doing prototypes and analysis is also something we should strive for in their goals and success. This will help incentivize and motivate them to also feel good in working and thinking in a disruptive way and thus have a common goal as you.

Conclusion

With this chapter, we reach the end of the book and the journey of AI transformation as well. We started by learning about the world view, how AI is coming along in various fields, how to go about preparing oneself and their team in the direction of the momentum, and towards the end, we learned a few ways to get the innovation and evolution on autopilot for the future. The book attempted to provide clarity and actionable steps for the managers to find direction in this sweeping wave of AI, which is transforming everything around us. We hope that this text turns out to be useful for your journey to become a better leader, even in the wake of the uncertain, disruptive, but innovative new world powered by AI.

Join our Discord space

Join our Discord workspace for latest updates, offers, tech happenings around the world, new releases, and sessions with the authors:

https://discord.bpbonline.com

Index